What the Church Owes the Jew

Leslie B. Flynn

D1502814

MAGNUS PRESS

MAGNUS PRESS
P.O. Box 2666
Carlsbad, CA 92018

WHAT THE CHURCH OWES THE JEW
Copyright ©1998 Leslie B. Flynn

First Edition, 1998

Printed in the United States of America

Copyedited by Rose Hamill

ISBN 0-9654806-3-1

Publisher's Cataloging-in-Publication
(Provided by Quality Books, Inc.)

Flynn, Leslie B.
    What the church owes the Jew / by Leslie B. Flynn. —
    1st ed. p. cm. Includes bibliographical references.
    Preassigned LCCN: 98-67365 ISBN: 0-9654806-3-1

    1. Christianity and other religions—Judaism.
    2. Judaism—Relations—Christianity. I. Title.

BM535.F59 1998   261.2′6
                   QBI98- 1076

02 01 00 99 98 10 9 8 7 6 5 4 3 2 1

To Reg and Connie Gerig,
friends of college days,
and ever since.

Contents

Foreword

Founder of Jews for Jesus
Executive Director: 1973-1996
Board Member: 1973-Present

Dr. Leslie B. Flynn is well qualified to address the subject of the church's debt to the Jews. He recognizes the differing roles of Gentiles, the church, and Israel, God's ancient, yet continuing covenant people.

The author does not write of the Jewish people as the Israel of long ago and far away. For 40 years Dr. Flynn pastored a very active church at the edge of metropolitan New York. He not only successfully evangelized many Jewish people, but also served as pastor to some of the most distinguished Jewish Christians. He had a unique and distinct ministry in helping Grace Baptist Church of Nanuet to gain a genuine love for the Jewish people. This love for Israel, coupled with love for the Bible, strengthened the church and enabled it to minister to the whole community.

I must say, as founder of Jews for Jesus, one of the most forthright missions to the Jews, that most Jews who come to faith in Christ do so as a result of the witness of conventional Christians. These believers in Jesus attend ordinary churches and have committed themselves to Jewish people for the purpose of sharing the wonderful works of God through Y'shua (Jesus).

However, sometimes the culture which prevents Jewish people from considering Jesus as the Messiah also works against Jewish Christians when they try to fit into the church. Though Jewish theological objections may have been answered, problems of social indoctrination still exist. Failure to understand Jewish culture may keep many Jews from feeling comfortable among non-Jews, even if they are brothers and sisters in the faith.

This book is designed to motivate church-oriented Christians to feel and behave toward Jews in a Christian way. You will be surprised to read of the many things in science and art that Jews have contributed to the larger civilization. Though World Jewry numbers less than 13 million, Jews have set a track record in philanthropy, public service, medicine, and other sciences. American Jews have been prominent in building the communications industries. The author also tells of Jewish spiritual contributions that are overwhelming. We find out how God used the Jewish people to establish and bless the church.

What Dr. Flynn tells in this book becomes the intellectual and spiritual armament to do the work of evangelism under fire. One learns to appreciate the Jewish people and comes to understand how the Christian Church has affected the thinking of Jews both positively and negatively. The reader will discover the unique role that God has for the Jews as a people. Perhaps a good subtitle for this book would be *What Every Gentile Christian Needs to Know About God and the Jews*.

Introduction

In his 1998 book *The Gifts of the Jews*, author Thomas Cahill traces the cultural history of late twentieth-century Western people back to their ultimate source—the religious ideas of ancient Israel. The book is subtitled *How a Tribe of Desert Nomads Changed the Way Everyone Thinks and Feels.* How true that we, and especially the church, are deeply indebted to the Jews for so many of our underlying values today.

Reading this fascinating story of Jewish origins, I thought of my association with so many Jewish people during my 40 years as pastor of Grace Baptist Church in Nanuet, NY. I recalled over 60 Jewish friends who attended our services with some degree of regularity between 1949 and 1989, approximately 30 of whom became official members.

Perhaps our location helps explain this high number of Jewish congregants in a Gentile church. Nanuet is situated in Rockland County, less than 30 miles from New York City with its approximately two million Jews, many of whom have been moving to the suburbs. A recent item in our local newspaper under the heading, "Judaism in Rockland," listed these statistics: "Of 172 congregations, 51 are synagogues. Of 193,311 congregants, about 60,000 are Jews."

That's close to 30% in both cases. For years our county's public schools have closed for major Jewish holidays.

For two years before founding Jews for Jesus, Moishe Rosen was a member of our church, attending regularly with his family. Also, two top leaders of the Chosen People Ministries, Daniel Fuchs and Harold Sevener, were faithful members here. Even without any aggressive outreach program Jews just seemed to gravitate here, knowing they would find a welcome. Every now and again we did do something with our Jewish friends in mind. For example we offered a three-month course on "Jews and Christianity" in our Sunday school, taught by a Jewish Christian, with nearly 100 present each week. I recall one deacon remarking approvingly, "That hall looks like a synagogue!" One April we invited Chosen People Ministries to hold a Passover Seder in our facilities. Of the 250 present, over 50 were Jewish, many outsiders. One Sunday evening we had a round table discussion with twelve Jewish Christians on the platform.

I began to receive invitations to address Jewish-Christian organizations in the New York area. I'll never forget, back in the 60's, speaking at a family night at the Chosen Peoples' mission in Coney Island, led by Hilda Koser. What a thrill to see 60 people from children to seniors, all Jews and all Christians, singing hymns about Jesus! On at least three occasions I addressed this monthly family service, always relishing the evening.

When Jews for Jesus was conducting its early New York City crusades, I was often invited to bring a message of encouragement to the young missionaries before they ventured onto the streets of the Big Apple. But I was the one who received the inspiration—by just looking into the vibrant faces of 50 young people, all wearing a "Jews for Jesus" T-shirt and raring to get out midst the crowds to distribute their bag full of gospel broadsides.

IV

I recall speaking at the Friday night service at the nearby Chosen People headquarters, the Jews for Jesus Friday night service at the Taft Hotel in downtown New York, a neighboring Messianic congregation, the annual conference of the national Fellowship of Testimonies to the Jews, and twice to local Jewish synagogues to explain what Baptists believe. Often when I addressed Jewish groups I spoke on the church's debt to the Jews. I mentioned how anti-Semitism was so illogical and irrational, especially for Christians and churches who stopped to realize how much they owed Jewish people.

I also spoke on "What the Church Owes the Jew" in our local Sunday morning broadcast, making our customary offer of a free copy of the message to those writing in. A few weeks later, visiting those who had recently signed our church visitors' book, I knocked on the door of a man who immediately told me that he was Jewish, had heard my talk on the radio, had written for a copy, and had indeed been in church the previous Sunday, he now asked, "Would you give me permission to submit your talk to *Reader's Digest?*"

Laughingly I replied, "*Reader's Digest* would never print that!" He insisted on trying, so I said o.k. A few weeks later when the article came back from *Reader's Digest*, he phoned and asked if he could submit it to *Christian Life* magazine. Surprised that this Jewish gentleman knew about this Christian magazine, I asked, "Where did you ever hear about *Christian Life?*" He explained that he was in the business of selling mailing lists, including those of Christian magazines, immediately naming a few like *Moody, His,* and *Decision.* Then he repeated his request to be allowed to submit my pamphlet to *Christian Life.* I gave my permission. A few months later he phoned, to my amazement jubilantly informing me that the article had been accepted. It is this radio address and magazine article that became the springboard for this book with the same theme.

Looking back on my boyhood years, I often wonder if the Lord was preparing me to become the pastor of a church with so many Jewish adherents. On our street we had Jewish neighbors on both sides; to the north, the Cohens; to the south, the Kritzers, the Bricks, and the Spectors. My mother taught me never to make fun of Jews, as some did in our neighborhood, but impressed upon me that they were God's chosen people. "God will bless those that bless them," she would say, "and curse those that curse them."

Also, we attended a church where, as a boy, I heard our pastor say, "The Jews will be going back to their homeland some day." This was in the 1930s when such a possibility seemed remote. Every new pastor that followed through the years made the same prediction. It wasn't so surprising to me in 1948 when Israel became a nation, and Palestine her homeland.

My parents supported Jewish missions to the end of their days. I learned this on a visit to my home city of Hamilton, Ontario, Canada, after both my parents had passed away within a six-week period. When I stopped at a downtown Christian bookstore, which contained the Canadian office of Chosen People Ministries, the lady in charge told me that, just a week before my father entered the hospital in his final illness, he had come into the office with his monthly gift of $5 for the mission. It was late afternoon and the commute traffic had started. My father was a few weeks from his 90th birthday. He was blind in one eye, and a cataract was growing in the other. She said that he tapped his way along with a cane, trying to weave his way through the busy traffic. "At that point," said the lady, "I went out and guided him safely across. And reaching the office, he handed me his regular gift for Jewish missions."

How much we owe the Jews! The contents of this book reveal a huge debt which we can never begin to repay. However, in recognition of this indebtedness, I would like to offer this volume, insignificant contribution though it be, in partial repayment of my vast obligation.

1

Exploits Far Beyond
Their Number

A few years ago I was invited to speak in a Long Island home at a December Hanukkah party for Jews and Christians. Early in the evening the leader introduced a game involving two columns, one listing notable achievements, the other the names of well known persons. The idea was to match achievement with achiever. For example, polio with Jonas Salk; violin with Jascha Heifetz; conductor with Leonard Bernstein; composer with Irving Berlin; RCA with David Sarnoff; Atomic Energy Commission with Lewis Strauss; pianist with Artur Rubinstein; and British Prime Minister with Benjamin Disraeli. It soon dawned on those playing that every one in the list of notable achievers was Jewish.

Of five-and-a-half billion people on earth, less than fourteen million (one-fourth of 1%) are classified as Jews. One would think that their accomplishments would be minimal, but instead they greatly exceed the proportion to their numbers. More than 15% of Nobel prizes have gone to Jews since the program's inception in 1899. No other ethnic group can claim such a high ratio of winners.

Similarly, with six million Jews in the USA, comprising only 3% of the population, the extent and significance of their contributions are mindboggling. U.S. Jews are twice as likely to go to college than Gentiles, are five times more likely to be admitted to an Ivy School, and are over-represented in the fields of medicine, science, law, and dentistry.[1] In this chapter we shall mention the names of many well-known Jews and their exploits. These lists in various areas are by no means thorough, but rather illustrative of their widespread achievements.

MEDICINE

Until 40 years ago summer was the dread polio season. Though the end of the school year brought opportunity for sunshine and swimming, parents ordered children to avoid the public pool and the air-conditioned movie theater. Crowds were thought to be a likely place to catch the paralyzing poliomyelitis. Children were told to report immediately the slightest sore throat or the feared stiff neck. Yet little bodies filled hospital wards; 1952 reached a record 57,879 cases, all incurable. As a pastor, I recall making a hospital visit around that time to a young mother in an iron lung.

Then, in 1954, the National Foundation for Infantile Paralysis, with the aid of 75 million dimes collected in theaters countrywide, tested the first polio vaccine on nearly two million schoolchildren. On April 12, 1955, the vaccine's researcher announced that it worked. Within weeks children lined up by the thousands for the shots. The breakthrough brought relief from the annual summer dread. Though it's tragically possible for the live vaccine to cause the disease, the annual number of cases has dropped to a dozen or so. Polio has been virtually eradicated from the industrial world. And the man who discovered the vaccine was Jonas Salk, a Jew.

If an anti-Semitic decided to boycott all the tests and cures discovered by Jews, he would certainly open himself to a host of serious diseases. Besides refusing Jonas

Salk's polio vaccine, he would also decline the polio pill by Dr. Albert Sabin; the test to fight diphtheria invented by Bela Schick; the diet regime of Joseph Goldberger which has fought pellagra to a standstill; blood transfusions made possible by the work of Dr. E. J. Cohen of Harvard, who developed the methods of extracting blood plasma and gamma gobulin, saving tens of thousands of lives since the start of World War II; the Wassermann test for syphilis; Salvarsan, invented by Paul Ehrlich and the first cure for syphilis; the vaccine for hepatitis discovered by Baruch Blumberg; streptomycin discovered by Dr. Selman Abraham Waxman as an antibiotic for various bacteria including tuberculosis; chlorohydrate for convulsions discovered by Dr. J. Von Liebig; and vitamins discovered by Casimir Funk.

What a list of illnesses held in check by Jewish medical research: paralysis, diphtheria, pellagra, blood loss, syphilis, hepatitis, bacterial infections, convulsion, and nutritional deficiency. Gratefully we admit our medical debt to the Jews for healthier living.

In the area of mental health we recall the name of Sigmund Freud and his wife, Anna, who carried on his work. Here are a few well-known Jewish names in this field: Alfred Adler, Viktor Frankl, Eric Fromm, William Glasser, Abraham Maslow, and E. H. Erikson. Though we may disagree with their findings, we acknowledge their contributions.

MILITARY

In an article, "The Jews Among Us," the *Reader's Digest* points out that equality and freedom did not spring full-blown from America's soil to all new settlers.[2] When the earliest Jews arrived at New Amsterdam in 1654, Governor Peter Stuyvesant wanted to banish these 23 impoverished men, women, and children, and wrote the directors of the Dutch West India Co. in Holland for authority to do so. While the "wandering Jews" awaited a verdict, the captain of the ship held an auction of the newcomers' possessions to reimburse himself for the Jews' passage. The citizens of New Amsterdam bought these pitiful items, then to show direct disapproval of their governor's attitude, handed the money back as a gift to the Jews. Seven months later the governor received instructions to allow people freedom to follow "his own beliefs."

At the outbreak of the Revolutionary War in 1776, 122 years after the first Jews came to America, 2500 Jewish immigrants were scattered throughout the 13 colonies. The *Reader's Digest* reports that in the active fighting "the Jews produced three colonels and several score of majors, captains and lieutenants, while hundreds of others served in the front—a remarkable showing, in view of the fact that the total Jewish adult male population in all the colonies was barely 1000."[3]

As new streams of Jews immigrated from Germany, Russia, and Poland, their clothes, customs and language made them seem strange to other Americans. Though often discriminated against, Jews became a fully integrated part of the nation. When the Civil War broke out, Max I. Dimont says, "Southern rabbis exhorted Jews to volunteer for the Confederate Gray, and northern rabbis exhorted Jews to volunteer for the Union Blue. When the war was over, there were nine Jewish generals and hundreds of Jewish field officers in the Union Army. The count was proportionately the same in the Confederate Army."[4] A thousand Jews fought in the Battle of Gettysburg.

Jews have fought in all our wars since. According to the *Reader's Digest*, "In World War I they made up nearly 4.5 percent of our Armed Forces and their dead were five percent of the total, though Jews continued little more than three percent of our population. In World War II and again in Korea they made up 4.5 percent of the fighting forces while still 3.2 percent of our people." An estimated 10,000 Jews fought in Vietnam. The Jewish War Veteran's Association celebrated its centennial anniversary in 1996.

MUSIC

Darryl Lyman's book, *Great Jews in Music*, contains over one hundred major biographies and hundreds more thumbnail sketches focusing on the professional careers of Jewish musical artists.[5] This compendium shows how Jews have enriched literally every aspect of music.

The concert stage has been enhanced by the performances of pianists Vladimir Horowitz, Alexander Brailowsky, Artur Rubinstein, Vladimir Ashkenazy, Leon Fleisher, Myra Hess, George Antheil, and Leopold Godowsky.

Violinists include Isaac Stern, Jascha Heifetz, Nathan Milstein, Misha Diechter, Yehudi Menuhin, David Oistrakh, and Itzhak Perlman.

Composers embrace Harold Arlen, Ernest Bloch, Aaron Copland, Morton Gould, William Schuman, and Felix Mendelssohn who was baptized as a boy and raised a Lutheran. Known for his oratorio, *Elijah*, he was also a pianist and conductor.

Among Metropolitan Opera singers are Robert Merrill, Roberta Peters, Beverly Sills, Rise Stevens, and Richard Tucker.

Conductors include George Szell, Fritz Reiner, Eugene Ormandy, James Levine, Arthur Fiedler, Andre Kostelanetz, Serge Koussevitzky, and George Henschel.

Much of our popular music was written by Jerome Kern, Irving Berlin, Oscar Hammerstein II, Sigmund Romberg, George Gershwin, Richard Rodgers, Frank Loesser, and Larry Hart.

SPORTS

Three Jews who won baseball's Most Valuable Player Award were Hank Greenberg for the American League in 1935 and 1940; Al Rosen for the American League in 1953; and Los Angeles Dodger ace Sandy Koufax for the National League in 1963. Koufax also won *Sport* magazine's Most Valuable Player award in the World Series in 1963 and 1965. When Sandy Koufax refused to pitch the first game of the 1965 World Series because it was scheduled for Yom Kippur, he pitched next day and beat the Yankees. After that second game Yankee third-baseman Clete Boyer facetiously commented, "Why couldn't today have been a Jewish holiday?"

Benny Leonard, Barney Ross, Jackie Fields, Maxie Rosenblum, and Rudy Goldberg are among top Jewish boxers. Mark Spitz won the Associated Press Athlete of the Year Award in 1972 for his swimming prowess and winning Olympic performance. Mel Allen and Howard Cosell were well-known sportscasters, also Sid Luckman, a former football star as well. The Jewish Sports Hall of Fame, launched in 1978, is located in the Wingate Institute for Physical Education in Israel, and has a branch in Los Angeles. Within a few years its roster had climbed to 47 members.

SCIENCE, PHILOSOPHY, PUBLIC SERVICE, PHILANTHROPY, JOURNALISM

Dimont mentions a wide range of interests in which Jews have excelled.[6]

Sir William Herschel, the first to measure the distances of stars from the sun, also discovered the planet Uranus. Karl Schwarzschild contributed to the understanding of the internal composition of stars. Jewish chemists were the first to synthesize indigo, to produce ammonia, to determine the composition of chlorophyll and the role of enzymes in the chemical process of life.

Jewish physicists discovered the Hertzian wave, studied photoelectric phenomena, isolated isotopes, codiscovered gamma rays, and, led by Einstein who was famous for his theory of relativity, produced nuclear energy by fission and paved the way for space travel.

Karl Jacobi founded modern mathematical physics with his theories of dynamics and partial differential equations, and the theory of elliptic functions. George Cantor introduced the theory of transfinite numbers. Hermann Minkowski began the geometry of numbers and first formulated the concept of relativity of time and space. Tullio Levi-Civita helped formulate the absolute differential calculus which made possible the mathematics of general relativity. With Einstein, Albert A. Michelson and Isidor Rabi won the Nobel prize in physics.

The second American woman to make a flight into space was Jewish-born astronaut Judith Resnik. Chosen as one of the seven crew members, she drew the assignment of flight engineer on the ill-fated Challenger which exploded soon after takeoff in January, 1986.

Given their strong interest in education, it's not surprising that 32 Jews were counted on the faculty of Harvard University one recent year. Baruch Spinoza, probably the second greatest philosopher (following Descartes) in the course of rationalistic development of modern thinking, helped loosen philosophy from the hold of mysticism and open a door to modern science. Martin Buber developed existential philosophy.

Benjamin Disraeli is likely the most famous Jew of England. As Prime Minister he was instrumental in building the British Empire during the reign of Queen Victoria. Sir Rufus Isaacs, Chief Justice of England, served as Viceroy of India.

In the USA a recent Congress tabulated 8 senators and 32 representatives who were Jewish. From Jewish students of American law schools have come seven justices of the Supreme Court: Louis D. Brandeis, Benjamin N. Cardozo, Felix Frankfurter, Abraham Fortas, Arthur Goldberg, Ruth Ginsburg, and Stephen Breyer. Bernard Baruch was adviser to a long list of Presidents. David Lilienthal and Admiral L. Strauss have been chairmen of the Atomic Energy Commission. Oscar S. Strauss was the first Jew to serve in the Cabinet. Herbert H. Lehman served four terms as Governor of New York State, and later as a U.S. Senator. Henry Kissinger served as Secretary of State. In addition to adjudicating on the Supreme Court, Arthur Goldberg was Secretary of Labor and U.S. Ambassador to the United Nations. The elder Henry Morgenthau was appointed Ambassador to Turkey, one of 45 Jews who held major diplomatic posts. As chairman of the Federal Reserve Board since 1987, Alan Greenspan has orchestrated a delicate economic policy by determining if and by how much interest rates should be raised.

Jewish fortunes have been poured into philanthropy. Between 1848 and 1860 the Jewish people of New York City supported almost one hundred charitable institutions, approximately one half of such incorporated organizations, although Jews represented less than 5% of the city's total population. The "Jews' Hospital in New York," incorporated in 1852, and becoming the well-known Mt. Sinai Hospital in 1866, purposed to relieve human misery, and for years admitted more free patients than any other private association. During the 1880s nearly 90% of its patients were treated without charge.[7]

A young Jewish poet, Emma Lazarus, who died at 38, not only wrote about her love for this country, but donated time to working among the poor immigrants who landed at Ward's Island. Affixed to the Statue of Liberty in 1903 is a quote from her sonnet which reads in part, "Give me your tired, your poor...."

Columnists who have appeared regularly for many years include Art Buchwald, Ann Landers and her twin sister Abigail, and Dr. Joyce Brothers.

HUMOR

We are also indebted to Jews for their sense of humor. In June, 1986, writers, academics and comedians gathered to examine Jewish humor during a four-day international conference sponsored by Tel Aviv University at New York City's New School for Social Research. Dr. Avner Ziv, chairman of Tel Aviv's department of educational sciences and chairman of the conference, said, "Jews, with their long history of pogroms, persecutions and killings, have developed a sense of humor known around the world—that is one of the few positive stereotypes about us."

One professor pointed out that Jews can see good elements in seemingly negative stereotypes. He used the example of the popular "Jewish-American princess" jokes, citing the one about the man who dies and requests that his ashes be scattered over Bloomingdale's so that his wife will visit once in a while. "On the one hand it's biting," said the professor. "But on the other, it's a tribute to the fact that Jewish men pride themselves on being good providers and pampering their wives."

Concentration camp humor provided the escape hatch from the reality of incredible suffering for many. Humor enabled Viktor Frankl, a Jewish psychiatrist who lost his wife and children to the ovens, and who was reduced to nakedness and near starvation midst cold and snow, to live with tragedy without destroying his spirit. He wrote, "Humor was another of the soul's weapons in the fight for self-preservation. It is well known that humor, more than anything else in the human makeup, can afford an

9

aloofness and an ability to rise above any situation, even if only for a few seconds."[8]

One speaker at the convention said, "A wink at disaster, a wry twist in tragic circumstances—this is the essential element of Jewish humor." Another said, "There is a kind of self mockery, a gallows humor that is typically Jewish." Leo Rosten, author of *The Joys of Yiddish* said of Jewish humor, "It adores irony because the only way the Jews could retain their sanity was to view a dreadful world with sardonic eyes."[9]

The same principle applies when the situation is not so serious or tragic. A comedian who performed at the conference told a true story how on a recent visit to Israel he ran over a cat. "I'm sorry," he told the man who owned the cat. "Is there anything I can do?" The Israeli replied, without a flicker of expression, "Mister, you can catch mice."

Leo Rosten believes that Jewish humor is also partly a result of the Jews' intense preoccupation with language. "You must remember," he said, "that when 90% or more of Europe was illiterate, there wasn't a Jewish boy who couldn't handle at least three languages"—Yiddish, Hebrew and his native language.

Rosten, one of the foremost chroniclers of Jewish humor, said his favorite joke was about two women who meet on the street. "Oh, you're pregnant, Mazel tov!" says the first. "Are you expecting a boy or a girl?" "Certainly," says the second.

In his book, Rosten gives a list of phrases we've all heard or used which probably are traced in English to Jewish influences. Here are a few which so clearly convey nuances of affection, displeasure, emphasis, disbelief, cynicism, ridicule:

"Get lost."
"You should live so long."

"My son, the doctor."
"I need it like a hole in the head."
"It shouldn't happen to a dog."
"He knows from nothing."
"From that he makes a living."
"He's a regular genius."
"Go hit your head against the wall."
"You want it should sing too."
"On him it looks good."
"Wear it in good health."[10]

So many comedians have been Jewish. Again, without evaluating the content of their humor here is a sample list: Jack Benny, Milton Berle, Joey Bishop, George Burns, Red Buttons, Sid Caesar, Eddie Cantor, Charlie Chaplin, Buddy Hackett, George Jessel, Danny Kaye, Alan King, Bert Lahr, Sam Levenson, Jerry Lewis, the Marx Brothers, Henry Morgan, Phil Silvers, Martha Raye, Carl Reiner, Joan Rivers, and Ed Wynn.

BUSINESS

In the Middle Ages when oppression denied Jews various occupations and ownership of land, many turned to moneylending. Though the Roman Catholic church forbade the lending of money at interest, the Jewish Talmud, while prohibiting usury, allowed the practice of moneylending as an aid to business, much like modern banks, as long as the rate was permissible and non-excessive. Moneylending was perhaps the chief contribution by the Jews to medieval culture.

The rulers of 17th and 18th century Europe, sensing Jewish acumen in financial matters, created the office of Court Jew, a sort of forerunner of the Secretary of the Treasury or Chancellor of the Exchequer. Almost all the 200 principalities in the Holy Roman Empire after the Thirty

Years' War had a Court Jew. These officers were loyal to their prince, freely came and went, dined with the heads of state, often were granted titles. But they never forgot their fellowmen in the ghettos. Their vocation foreshadowed later banking institutions.

As Jews landed in America, many sought employment in the cities. More than half a million crowded into tenements on New York's lower East Side. They filled similar slums in Boston, Philadelphia, and Chicago. With the invention of the sewing machine in the 1840's, many found work in the garment industry.

Some went west to heed the call for farmers. Many with packs on their backs also headed west, peddling merchandise and saving their pennies to start some business enterprise. The peddler's display box became a dry goods store, and later a department store. Department stores or chains were founded or owned by Jews: Macy's, Gimbel's, Bloomingdale's, Niemann-Marcus, Sears and Roebuck, E.J. Korvette's, Filene's, Stern's, Saks, Ohrbach's, Abraham and Straus.[ll]

Through the years Jewish Americans entered most every industry. Charles Fleischmann succeeded in the yeast-making business. Hirsch Manischewitz started Manischewitz Foods. Bennett Cerf, Elmer Adler, and Donald Klopper began Random House publishing company. Samuel Rosoff constructed many of New York's subways, while Louis J. Horowitz built many of the city's skyscrapers. Richard Simon and M.M. Schuster were founders of Simon and Schuster Publishing Co. The Guggenheims had a major part in the development of copper mining. Adolph Ochs, publisher of the *New York Times*, made it one of the world's leading newspapers. Katharine Graham served long as Chairman of the Washington Post Co. For years Gerald Swope presided over General Electric, David Sarnoff over RCA, and William Paley over CBS.

Especially in the motion picture industry were Jews willing to take pioneering financial risks. William Fox founded 20th Century-Fox; Sam Goldwyn, Louis B. Mayer, and Marcus Lowe, M-G-M; Carl Laemmle, Universal; Harry M. Warner, Warner Brothers; Harry Cohn, Columbia Pictures; and Adolph Zukor, Paramount.

Theatergoers have applauded the plays of George S.Kaufman, Lillian Hellman, Elmer Rice, Irwin Shaw, Moss Hart, S.N. Behrman, Arthur Miller, Clifford Odets, Sydney Kingsley, and Irwin Shaw.

Actors on stage, radio, and TV abound, such as Peter Falk, Jack Lord, and Dustin Hoffman. A recent producer with great success, Steven Spielberg filmed Schindler's List.

In the fall of 1996, 18 eminent Jewish Americans traveled to Ellis Island—among them playwright Arthur Miller, Justice Ruth Bader Ginsburg and Olympic swimmer Mark Spitz—to pose in a specially constructed labyrinth against a backdrop of Manhattan's skyline, for French photographer, Frederic Brenner, to include in his new book *Jews/America/A Representation*. Brenner, who has traveled to 37 countries to photograph Jews, comments, "In America they aren't merely in the mainstream, they create it."[12]

A Jewish merchant, wearing his yarmulke and holding his bag of goods, was headed home to New England on a crowded train. The only empty seat was beside him. Passengers boarding the train avoided sitting there. Finally a reluctant salesman, unable to find any other spot, sat next to the Jew. After an awkward silence the salesman said, "I come from a village up in Maine and I'm proud to say there are no Jews there."

"A village, you say," came the merchant's reply. "That's because there are no Jews."

Whether or not the presence of Jews spurs a village, town or city to grow and succeed, society owes many of its scientific and cultural advances to Jews. Because of

13

these valuable contributions the church also has benefited in numerous ways. In the medical field alone missionaries, pastors, leaders, and lay members have been spared serious illness through early diagnosis, or have been nursed back to health through medicines discovered by Jewish doctors and scientists, providing them with the freedom and longevity to continue their ministries.

Church people have also profited from Jewish interest in culture. Jews have endowed university chairs in the arts, given millions for the erection of concert auditoriums and museums, come to the financial rescue of opera companies and symphony orchestras, and donated spectacular collections of paintings and other art works to museums. Names like the Guggenheims, the Rosenwalds, the Strauses, the Warburgs, and the Schiffs are bywords in the promotion of the arts. In His common grace God not only makes the sun to rise and the rain to fall everywhere, but He has also given to all people the enjoyment of beautiful music, painting, and drama. Much of the art church people enjoy comes to them because of the Jews.

For these scientific and aesthetic gifts we are deeply indebted. However, as notable and numerous these contributions are, the greatest heritage of the Jews to the church is spiritual. The next six chapters will explore six spiritual legacies basic to the church's very existence and to its ongoing ministry to God's world.

NOTES

1. David Larsen, *Jews, Gentiles, and the Church* (Grand Rapids: Discovery House, 1995), p. 81.

2. Albert Q. Maisel, *Reader's Digest*, April 1955, pp. 26-31.

3. Ibid.

4. Max I. Dimont, *Jews, God and History* (New York: Signet Books, 1962), p. 360.

5. Darryl Lyman, *Great Jews in Music* (Middle Village, New York: Jonathan David Publishers, 1986).

6. Dimont, pp. 336-338.

7. David A. Rausch, *Friends, Colleagues, and Neighbors* (Grand Rapids: Baker Book House, 1996), p. 19.

8. Viktor Frankl, *Man's Search for Meaning* (New York: Washington Square Press, 1946), p. 66.

9. Leo Rosten, *The Joys of Yiddish* (New York: Pocket Books, 1970), preface, p. xvii.

10. Ibid., preface, pp. xiii, xiv.

11. Ron Landau, *The Book of Jewish Lists* (New York: Stein and Day, 1982), pp.140-141.

12. *Newsweek*, September 30, 1996, p. 62.

2

The World's Best Seller

Since the invention of printing in the 15th century, the Bible has been the world's best seller generation after generation. Even during Hitler's regime in Germany sales of Bibles easily outstripped those of his own book, *Mein Kampf*. In a recent year roughly 60 million Bibles were distributed worldwide, plus 90 million New Testaments and 1,650 million portions of Scripture.

The most universal book of all times, the Bible has been translated into more languages than any other book. The complete Bible is now in 342 languages, the New Testament in 823, and portions in 957, making a grand total of 2,122 languages which now have some Scripture. Translation work is going on in 1,678 other languages. And this book which outsells and outcirculates all other books is a Jewish book.

Approximately 40 authors wrote its 66 books. All these authors, except Luke, were Jews. God used Jewish minds, Jewish emotions, and Jewish styles to pen the Scriptures. Holy men of God wrote as they were inspired by the Holy Spirit. And these holy men were Jews.

THE OLD TESTAMENT

Moses, spared from drowning by divine providence and trained in Pharaoh's palace in all the wisdom and learning of Egypt, became the liberator and lawgiver of God's chosen people. He was also the author of the first five books of the Old Testament.

Moses began Genesis with the record of creation. After the accounts of the fall, flood, and dispersion of the nations at Babel, Moses told of God's call to Abraham, Isaac, and Jacob to be the patriarchs of His chosen people. Since Jacob was also named Israel, this new nation was known as the children of Israel, composed of his twelve sons and their descendants. Later, Israelites were also called "Hebrews" and "Jews." Moses traced their history into Egypt, their escape from slavery through the Red Sea, and their 40-year wilderness wanderings.

Later Jewish authors wrote of the conquest of Canaan; the disobedience and repentance of the Israelites during the days of the judges; the united kingdom; the division of Israel into the ten tribes of the north and the two tribes of Judah and Benjamin in the south; the repeated idolatry which sent both kingdoms into captivity; and the return of a remnant from exile to resettle their promised land.

Throughout ancient Israel's long history, Jewish writers penned the Old Testament's wisdom literature. King Solomon and many others shared thoughts and ideas about God and life, eternal concepts still treasured today by people everywhere.

In difficult times we turn to one of the wisdom books, the Psalms, for comfort, guidance and strength. Approximately half of these 150 poems were composed by David. Who isn't familiar with his immortal 23rd Psalm? This sweet singer was a Jew, the shepherd-boy who became the second king of Israel.

The last seventeen books of the Old Testament bear the names of 16 Jewish prophets. Outstanding among them is Isaiah, who painted the portrait of the coming Man of Sorrows (chapter 53).

PRESERVATION OF THE OLD TESTAMENT

God not only inspired the Old Testament, but preserved it as well. Faithfully copied by Jewish scribes from ancient days, a guild of trained Jewish scholars, known as the Masoretes, took over the work in the 6th century A.D. To insure microscopic accuracy in copying the text, these scholars used many checks and counterchecks. For example, they counted the number of words on a page and noted the middle word. Though not faultless, today's standard Masoretic Text of the Old Testament agrees remarkably with Hebrew scrolls of the Old Testament found among the Dead Sea Scrolls. What other literature has been so faithfully preserved?

Malcolm Muggeridge, famed British writer and TV personality, related a modern counterpart (on a much smaller scale) involving a faithful Ukrainian pastor who showed him a whole Bible which had been beautifully and meticulously copied out by some of his compatriots to use in their clandestine worship. Said Muggeridge, "I thought of these secret believers toiling away night after night at their task, and reflected that in all history there was no other written matter whose reproduction by such arduous means and in such hazardous circumstances could conceivably have seemed worthwhile. Would similar risks have been taken and similar loving care expended on copying out, say, the Magna Carta if for some reason it had become unobtainable? Or the American Declaration of Independence? Or the Communist Manifesto?....Or the Thoughts of Chairman Mao?....The very suggestion is preposterous."[1]

Only the Bible has received such careful preservation.

When the church was born, it assumed the sacredness of the Scriptures of Judaism, and found in those same Scriptures the foundation of its own faith. The church understood itself in the light of the Old Testament. Convinced that Jesus was the final completion of the law and the prophets, believers ransacked the Scriptures for any foreshadowing of the fulfillment of divine revelation.

This linkage of Old and New Testaments led many Jews to faith. But later when Gentiles began to predominate in the churches, this kind of handling of their sacred books angered some Jews who accused Gentile Christians of stealing their Old Testament. Christians would reply that because their faith was rooted in the Old Testament, these writings were precious to them as well. Gentiles should recognize their debt to the Jews for the Bible. One minister in New York City, whenever he read an Old Testament passage from the pulpit, would refer to the text as "the Scriptures of the Jews."

THE NEW TESTAMENT

A young Jewess who began to attend our church told me how a fellow-employee had jogged her interest in Christianity, in spite of the advice of her family to leave Jesus to the Gentiles. She said, "I opened my heart and earnestly listened as he took me through the Old Testament and showed me how various verses had been completed in the New Testament. Up until then, I had been under the mistaken notion that the two were separate books—the Old Testament for the Jews and the New Testament for Gentiles. But he showed me that the New Testament authors were Jewish. After weeks of discussion, I remember going to a bookstore in New York City to purchase my first Bible. Even then, I was so skeptical—I spent over an hour going through various verses comparing a Jewish Bible on the shelf with a New American Standard Bible which had been recommended to me. Finally, satisfied in my mind that the recommended Bible was authentic, I purchased it and placed a fabric cover over it to prevent my parents from finding out. Many hours were spent in my room behind closed doors plowing through the pages." She came to faith in Jesus as her Messiah, and married a Christian man.

The New Testament is just as much a piece of Jewish literature as the Old Testament. Of the eight named authors of the 27 New Testament books: Matthew, Mark, Luke, John, Paul, James, Peter and Jude, all are Jewish except the Gentile physician, Luke (Col. 4:10-14).

Almost half of the New Testament books, 13 of 27, were written by Paul. Who was this one-time murderer of Christians? He informs us that he came from untainted Jewish ancestry, "circumcised on the eighth day, of the people of Israel, of the tribe of Benjamin, a Hebrew of Hebrews; in regard to the law, a Pharisee; as for zeal, persecuting the church; as for legalistic righteousness, faultless" (Phil. 3:5,6). Though he became known as the apostle to the Gentiles, Paul possessed fervent love for "those of my own race, the people of Israel" (Rom. 9:3,4). He said that from them came the covenants and the receiving of the law. Indeed we are in debt to the Jews for the entire Bible, both Old and New Testaments. The Bible has been so carefully transmitted and well preserved through history that Frederic Kenyon, renowned paleographer and textual critic, affirmed that "The Christian can take the whole Bible in his hand and say without fear or hesitation that he holds in it the true Word of God, handed down without essential loss from generation to generation throughout the centuries."[2]

THE BIBLE HAS DEEPLY INFLUENCED ENGLISH-SPEAKING CULTURE

English literature

Dr. William Lyon Phelps, once professor of English at Yale University, said that "The Bible has been a greater influence on the course of English literature than all other forces put together."[3]

Who can appreciate Milton's *Paradise Lost*, Bunyan's

Pilgrim's Progress, da Vinci's *Last Supper,* Mendelsohn's *Elijah,* Haydn's *Creation* and Handel's *Messiah* apart from a knowledge of the Bible?

Dr. Lawrence E. Nelson, former Director of the Division of Languages at the University of Redlands, wrote a book *Our Roving Bible,* in which he traces the influence of the Bible on the writings of our great poets and authors. His book is the source of many of the following facts.[4]

In *The Canterbury Tales* Chaucer's (1340-1400) characters show deep, almost appalling familiarity with Scripture. In two prose tales alone Chaucer referred to 160 Bible passages, quoted from 40 books of the Bible and Apocrypha, and mentioned by name, from one to 20 times each, 60 biblical persons.[5]

New combinations of words were introduced into the English language by Tyndale's (1492-1536) translation of the Bible, including "beautiful," "peacemaker," "broken-hearted," "longsuffering," "stumblingblock," "scapegoat," and "filthy lucre." Coverdale's (1488-1568) Bible initiated new coalitions of words such as "lovingkindness," "tender mercy," "noonday," "bloodguiltiness," "morning star," and "kindhearted."[6]

In Shakespeare's (1564-1616) 37 plays are found over a thousand allusions to 36 books of the Bible[7]

John Milton's (1608-1674) *Paradise Lost* rests heavily on the vision of the heavenly city in Revelation 21 and 22.

John Bunyan (1628-1688), jailed for preaching outside the Church of England, immersed himself in the Scriptures until he became a walking Bible. His *Pilgrim's Progress,* an allegory of a spiritual journey termed by the *London Times* "the world's best supplement to the Bible," had an unparalleled sale of over a hundred thousand copies during his life, and was later translated into over a hundred languages.[8]

Charles Dickens (1812-1870) drew upon the Bible in his novels to the tune of 365 quotations.[9]

In four of Thomas Hardy's (1840-1928) novels, 132 passages, in an incomplete counting, were found to be influenced by the Bible. Names of some of his characters betray a scriptural origin: Jacob Smallbury, Joseph Poorgrass, Reuben Dewy, Cain Ball, Benjamin Pennyways, Laban Tall, Mark Clark, Matthew Moon, Andrew Randle, Bathsheba Everdene, and Susanna Bridehead.[10]

Over a thousand biblical references occur in the writings of England's Poet Laureate Lord Tennyson (1850-1892).[11]

American literature

The New England Primer, the outstanding textbook in U.S. history, dominated American education for over a century, selling in a meager market an astonishing seven million copies before 1840. With 85% of its contents biblical, it was called the "Little Bible of New England." Letters of the alphabet were taught thus, for "A", "In Adam's fall, we sinned all."

In the writings of essayist Ralph Waldo Emerson (1803-1882), chapter and verse have been cited for 529 references.[12]

In 285 poems of John Greenleaf Whittier (1807-1892) are 816 passages taken directly or indirectly from the Bible.[13]

Intimacy with the Bible was a strong factor in novelist Harriet Beecher Stowe's (1811-1896) *Uncle Tom's Cabin.*[14]

A biographer of John Ruskin (1819-1900) in a cursory count found 4800 quotations from the Bible in his writings.[15]

Though Walt Whitman (1819-1892) claimed freedom from borrowings, researchers in his poems tallied 197 allusions, paraphrases, and quotations (including 37 repetitions) from the Bible, plus 97 other more generalized ones.[16]

Herman Melville (1819-1891), author of *Moby Dick*, favored the Old Testament, which provided two-thirds of the 650 biblical references in his writings, including allusions to more than 100 biblical characters. Jonah is the most mentioned, then Adam, Jesus, Noah, Solomon, Job, Abraham, Moses, and Paul.[17]

As early as 1931 the New York Public Library issued a list of 1,948 plays based on the Bible, mostly by English authors. In six issues during a two-year period ten popular magazines, including *Cosmopolitan, Ladies' Home Journal, Saturday Evening Post, Good Housekeeping, Life,* and *Time* quoted, referred to or alluded to the Bible over 1310 times.[18]

For centuries the Bible has enriched our language, ennobled our literature, and inspired our souls. Spurgeon noted, "A Bible which is falling apart usually belongs to someone who is not."

And this Bible is a Jewish book.

Everyday speech

Because of the Bible's sheer literary value, a large number of its phrases have found their way into everyday speech. Many have a catchy ring whose scriptural origin people often fail to recognize. What a remarkable book to possess so many expressions which, though centuries old, are still heard in the conversations of today's taxi drivers and office workers.

Here are some: "root of the matter," "the fat of the land," "feet of clay," "a good old age," "die before his time," "gives up the ghost," "set his house in order," "a man after my own heart," "apple of his eye," "wit's end," "rise and shine," "spare the rod," "see eye to eye," "holier than thou," "come now, and let us reason together," "birds of the air," "broken reed," "clear as crystal," "decently and in order," "handwriting on the wall," "highways and hedges," "holy of holies," "labor of love," "lick the dust," "loaves and fishes," "many mansions," "peace on earth," "pride of life," "salt of the earth," "a soft answer," "still small voice," "thorn in the flesh," "weighed in the balances," "whited sepulchers," "widow's mite," "windows of heaven," "wings of the morning," "gall and wormwood," "by the skin of our teeth," "by the sweat of our brow," "strain out a gnat" "the spirit is willing," "judge not," "sow the wind and reap the whirlwind," "valley of the shadow," "putting your candle under a bushel," "hiding your talent," "casting your pearls before swine," "let not the sun go down upon your wrath," "day of judgment," "land of milk and honey," "the promised land, "cup of cold water," "the eye of the needle," "the mote in your eye," "first fruits," "the strait and narrow way," and "on wings of eagles."

Many puns would not be comprehended apart from a biblical base. Pedestrians crossing a busy corner are called "the quick and the dead." Jesus' question is rendered, "What shall it profit a man if he gain a telescope and lose his sight?" English statesman Sir Thomas More could prove his own genealogy with the quip, "Noah had three sons, Shem, Ham, and one More." Because Mount Holyoke Seminary supplied so many missionaries' wives, it was dubbed a "Missionary Rib Factory."

Names

About one thousand communities in the U.S. have names which came from the Bible. The alphabetical list extends from Aaron in Kentucky to Zion in Arkansas, and according to the *National Zip Code Directory*, includes, among others: Ararat, Athens, Asher, Alexandria, Antioch, Bethel, Bethlehem, Beulah, Babylon, Berea, Bethesda, Bethany, Bethpage, Cana, Canaan, Carmel, Corinth, Dothan, Damascus, Dorcas, Eden, Elim, Ebenezer, Ephrata, Goshen, Gilead, Galatia, Hebron, Horeb, Jericho, Jordan, Joppa, Kidron, Lebanon, Memphis, Mizpah, Moriah, Macedon, Mount Hermon, Mount Horeb, Mount Olive, Mount Zion, Mount Calvary, Nazareth, Ninevah, Nebo, Olivet, Philadelphia, Pisgah, Philippi, Rehoboth, Rome, Salem, Sharon, Sodom, Syria, Saint John, Saint Paul, Sarepta, Sardis, Sidon,

Smyrna, Shiloh, Siloam, Sinai, Tekoa, Tabor, Zion. Many names appear in more than one state.

Many hospitals have biblical names like Mt. Sinai, St. Luke, Good Samaritan, St. Joseph, St. Mary, and St. Peter.

For centuries parents have given their offspring Bible names like Jesse, Daniel, Ezekiel, Lydia, Nathan, Naomi, Mary, Joseph, Abraham, Isaac, Jacob, Joseph, Moses, Aaron, Benjamin, Ruth, Solomon, David, Samuel, Saul, Paul, Timothy, Titus, Silas, Seth, Noah, Jonah, Stephen, Priscilla, Elizabeth, Lois, Hannah, Eunice, Josiah, Philip, and the names of the apostles. Around 1300 A.D. one Englishman of every five was named "John".

In Puritan days parents affixed to their helpless children names like Abimilech, Habakkuk, Hezekiah, Melchizedek, Shadrach, Zebulon, and Zerubbabel. Other names were Be-Stedfast, Faint not, Fear-not, Flee-fornication, and Good-gift. Such names have long since faded from birth records. Names of virtues like Charity, Faith, and Hope are now much less frequent. Today, unfortunately, more likely are the names of movie stars and other celebrities.

LIKE NO OTHER BOOK, THE BIBLE HAS WITHSTOOD THE OPPOSITION OF ITS ENEMIES, AND THE CARELESSNESS OF ITS FRIENDS

The attacks of its enemies

No book has suffered such onslaughts as the Bible. In 303 A.D. Roman Emperor Diocletian ordered Bibles burned, but the next emperor, Constantine, enthroned the Bible as the judge of truth.

In 1414 an English law declared that all who read the vernacular Bible would forfeit land, cattle, goods and life. At one time printing the Bible in common English was illegal and dangerous. Tyndale, who vowed to get the Bible into the hands of every person in England, even the man behind the plow, was forced to flee to the continent where he printed Bibles and smuggled them into England in bales of cloth and sacks of flour. Unable to keep them out, bishops of the Church of England piled them in heaps and burnt them publicly. During door-to-door searches for Bibles, housewives hid copies in hollowed-out loaves of bread in the ovens. Tyndale was hunted, betrayed, and burned at the stake.

Despite imperial orders for its destruction in various countries and at different times, this Jewish book has managed to outlive all the kings and tyrants who issued such decrees.

The carelessness of printers

In addition to the attacks by outside enemies, the Bible has suffered at the hands of careless printers who have given some strange spins to the language of the Bible. Such mistakes go almost unnoticed in lesser works of literature, but because the Bible has enjoyed such wide circulation in so many translations and editions, these printing blunders have received wide notoriety. Typos and odd translations have given us a list of amusing bloopers, provocative titles, and collector's items.

The "Wife-Beaters Bible" (1540) carries a printer's note beside I Peter 3 "to beat the fear of God into her head." The Geneva Bible (1560) was also known as the "Breeches Bible," because it clothes Adam and Eve with trousers. Genesis 3:7 is rendered, "They sewed fig leaves together and made themselves 'breeches'" instead of "aprons" as in the later King James. (The Geneva Bible was brought to America by the Pilgrims aboard the Mayflower because they rejected the King James Version as a "newfangled" and unacceptable translation.)

The first edition of the King James Bible is sometimes known as the "Great He Bible" because it says in Ruth 3:15, after a romantic episode, that "he (Boaz) went into the city."

The second edition correctly reads, "she (Ruth) went into the city," and is known as the "Great She Bible."

The "Judas Bible" (1611) has Judas, instead of Jesus, accompanying the disciples to the Garden of Gethsemane.

The famous "Wicked Bible" (1631) made the seventh commandment to say, "Thou shalt commit adultery." King Charles was so furious at this blunder that he ordered all copies destroyed and the printers heavily fined.

Around that time the "Fool's Bible" omitted "no" in Ps. 14:1, making it read, "The fool said in his heart there is a God." This error also cost the printer a substantial fine.

The "Unrighteous Bible" (1653) lightheartedly proclaimed that "the unrighteous shall inherit the kingdom of God."

More than 8,000 copies of the "Sin on Bible," the first English Bible printed in Ireland (1716), were distributed before the error was discovered and the words of Jesus to the women taken in adultery were correctly changed from "Sin on" to "Sin no more."

In the early 1700s a Boston printer forged the royal imprint on 1,000 copies of a Bible printed by John Baskett. This edition was so full of mistakes that it was nicknamed "A Baskett-ful of Errors." This same edition contained a new parable called "The Parable of the 'Vinegar'" instead of the "Vineyard." So this Bible received the dubious distinction of a second title, the "Vinegar Bible."

The "Denial Bible" (1792) says that Philip, not Peter, would deny Jesus three times.

The "Murderers Bible" (1801) has the book of Jude referring to "murderers" instead of "murmurers." Though this was rectified, the second edition had Numbers 35:18 reading, "The murderer shall surely be put 'together'" instead of "to death." Though this inaccuracy was corrected, the third edition kept the deadly theme going by making Mark 7:27 read, "Let the children first be 'killed'" instead of "filled."

The "Standing Fishes Bible" (1806) says "the 'fishes' shall stand when Ezekiel says "fishers" (47:10).

The "Camels Bible" (1832) says that when Rebekah was preparing for the trip to meet Jacob with her retinue of servants, she left the family tent with her "camels" instead of "damsels" (Genesis 24:61).

Though misprints dogged Bible publishing for centuries, maybe David summed it best when the "Printers Bible" has him exclaim, "Printers (instead of "princes") have persecuted me without cause" (Ps. 119:161).

Despite all the external opposition to the Bible through the centuries from its enemies, and all the printing mistakes from its friends, the Bible still survives as the greatest book of all time. And this book is a Jewish book.

THE BIBLE IN TODAY'S MEDIA

During a recent period I looked for allusions to the Bible in newspapers, radio and TV programs. Here are a few:

A journalist likened a crime-ridden city to Sodom and Gomorrah.

When the New York Mets were doing poorly one summer, a sportswriter tried to rally the fans. Sensing the seeming impossibility of his task, he wrote, "O ye of little faith."

In a *20-20* TV report on a new drug, one participant reported that now and again it had a Lazarus effect—that of giving new life. Again, when a biologist claimed he had restored 30-million-year-old bacteria to life, the *New York Times* on its front page called its revival "Lazarus-like."

When a female Miami lawyer was permitted to visit her native Cuba and planted a kiss on Castro's cheek during an interview, anti-Castro Cubans in Florida called it a "Judas kiss."

Before a NBA final championship game both coaches gave the players a day off. A sportswriter, on a takeoff of the seventh day of creation in Genesis 1, commented, "And on Monday neither the Knicks nor the Rockets rested."

In a baseball game when New York beat Boston, the sports page spoke of "Yankee pitchers grinding Red Sox bats into plowshares."

During the World Soccer Cup games the U.S.-Brazil contest was described as a "David versus Goliath" matchup.

When millions fled Rwanda, the press called it "an exodus of biblical sweep."

When a crowd of actors tried out for parts in a play, a theatre critic remarked, "Many are called, but who'll be chosen?"

A huge explosion of a gas-line in Edison, N.J., "brought a sense of Armageddon."

When a brother killed his brother, the story was captioned, "Modern story of Cain and Abel."

A *New York Times* editorial, suggesting that a certain leader bring his practice into line with his preaching, was headed, "Physician, Heal Thyself."

In a newspaper article on polls and their accuracy, the writer said that because those polled often did not know the facts, it became a case of "the blind leading the blind."

When the New York Rangers hockey team won the Stanley Cup, the sport pages quipped, "Their cup runneth over."

In a *Newsweek* article on the possibility of Senator Dole's running for the presidency in the 1996 elections, the article was titled, "Make a Doleful Noise."

A cover *Newsweek* story on stress was captioned, "A Nation of The Quick and The Dead-Tired."

When Judge Ito made a decision in a difficult ruling at the O.J. Simpson trial, a lawyer reacted, "He's trying to cut the baby in half." This was a reference to Solomon's problem of deciding which of two mothers was the real parent of one surviving baby.

On one TV program, the group of all those high-priced lawyers present in Judge Ito's court was likened to "that menagerie that even Solomon could not have presided over".

An ad in United Airlines Hemisphere magazine said, "If Hawaii is Paradise, Kauai is the Garden of Eden." An article on agriculture in the same issue was titled "Our Daily Bread."

Newsweek referred to President Clinton's Syria trip as "On The Road To Damascus."

Speaking of two men in conflict, New York Mayor Guiliani and New York Governor Pataki, the *New York Times* said, "Neither man will turn the other cheek."

During the days when the newly-empowered Republicans were passing bill after bill over futile Democrat opposition, one newspaper read, "After more Republican legislation angering Democrats, there will be wailing and gnashing of teeth."

Speaking of police attempts to stop panhandling down in the New York subways, a radio announcer began, "Ask and ye shall receive. There's less of that going on these days."

Reporting the return of basketball superstar Michael Jordan after a stint in pro baseball, *Newsweek* put it, "Archangel Michael's return is a 3-pointer at the buzzer. Roll, Jordan roll."

In the popular TV program, *Murder, She Wrote,* suddenly the lights went out, and someone exclaimed, "Let there be light."

A scene in Tom Clancy's bestselling novel *Debt of Honor* depicts the troubled faces of a board of directors at a time of crisis. Their first action was to vote in a former business associate as managing director and president. Many of the board looked to this visitor "as though he were Jesus come to clean out the temple" (Putnam, 1994, p.422).

31

At a memorial service after Israel's Prime Minister's assassination, his granddaughter movingly eulogized him as "the pillar of fire."

According to the *Guinness Book of Records*, the world's oldest set of triplets, and the first on record to reach age 95, live in a nursing home in Texas. In 1944 Charity Cardwell, in a wheelchair, led a reporter right over to two other women, also in wheelchairs. "This is Faith," she said, introducing her sister. Then, "This is Hope." Then, "I'm Charity." Pausing for effect, she added, "But the greatest of these is Charity."

The film "Chariots of Fire" derives its title from the Biblical episode of Elijah carried to heaven in a chariot of fire.

Pondering the penalty the Nevada State Athletic Commission would mete to Mike Tyson after he bit off part of Holyfield's ear in a world's heavyweight boxing championship bout in the summer of 1997, *Newsweek* reported that the public appeared "to desire almost Biblical retribution—perhaps an ear for an ear."

During Easter week of 1998, New York City's Cardinal O'Connor criticized big league baseball executives for having scheduled games on Good Friday. One newspaper headline read, "Sermon on the Mound."

This sampling, extracted from a recent period, shows how the Bible has infiltrated modern culture. This literary masterpiece of the ages we owe to the Jews. The Apostle Paul wrote to the Romans that the Jews "have been entrusted with the very words of God" (3:2).

The Bible is so important to the church because it provides a rule of faith and practice—what to believe and how to behave. The creedal articles of major denominations universally assert in one form or another that the Holy Bible is divinely inspired, a perfect treasure of instruction for godly living, with God for its author, salvation for its end, and truth for its matter, revealing the principles by which we will be judged. It is the supreme standard by which all human conduct, creeds, and opinions should be tried.

The Bible contains the message which the church is commissioned to proclaim, and which promises pardon for the penitent, encouragement for the troubled, and a pillow of hope for the perishing. What a debt the church owes the Jew!

NOTES

1. "The Book That Burns," *Eternity,* April 1977, p. 14.
2. Frederic Kenyon, quote in Philip W. Comfort, *The Complete Guide to Bible Versions* (Wheaton: Tyndale, 1996), pp. 32-33.
3. William Lyon Phelps, *Reading the Bible* (New York: Macmillan Co., 1919), p. 17.
4. Lawrence E. Nelson, *Our Roving Bible* (Nashville: Abingdon Cokesbury, 1945).
5. Ibid., p. 35.
6. Ibid., pp. 57-58.
7. Ibid., p. 62.
8. Ibid., pp. 99-101.
9. Ibid., p. 184.
10. Ibid., pp. 185, 187.
11. Ibid., p. 173.
12. Ibid., p. 159.
13. Ibid., p. 176.
14. Ibid., p. 178.
15. Ibid., p. 90.
16. Ibid., p. 156.
17. Ibid., p. 162.
18. Ibid., p. 228.

3

Knowledge Of
The One True God

On a round-the-world trip a few years ago, some missionaries in the Far East took us into one of their country's temples on a busy, crowded, sacred holiday. We saw people walk reverently up to a large idol, bow, and then drop "make believe" money into a fire on the altar. Others brought real fruit and vegetables to offer to their gods.

It's hard to be an atheist. Mankind everywhere has an idea, however inadequate, of a supreme being. Looking around at creation, a person reasons, "There must be a creator." Or seeing the marvelous structure of the human body, concludes, "There must be a designer." As Paul wrote, "For since the creation of the world God's invisible qualities—his eternal power and divine nature—have been clearly seen, being understood from what has been made..." (Rom. 1:20). The Bible never tries to prove the existence of God, but just assumes it in its opening verse, "In the beginning God..." (Gen. 1:1). God's existence seems to be an innate concept.

So, it's almost impossible to rid oneself of belief in the existence of a supreme being. Attempting to suppress the idea is like stopping a pendulum at the end of its motion to keep it from swinging back. The minute you relax your vigil, the pendulum returns. Like the atheist who in an off-guarded moment insisted, "There is no God, God knows."

Because mankind must worship something, but possesses seriously defective views of deity, people in various parts of the world have venerated gods for thousands of years that are many and varied, embracing animism, fetishism, pantheism, henotheism, and polytheism. At some time or other, societies have worshiped the sun, moon, stars, spirits, trees, and animals, including dogs, serpents, vermin, cows, rats, and fish.

How is it, then, that most of us who worship a supreme being do not bow down to worship idols with eyes that see not, ears that hear not, and mouths that speak not? Why is it that millions of people are *monotheists?* The answer is— God gave to the Jews the knowledge of the one true God. It was to them He said, "Hear, O Israel: The Lord our God, the Lord is one" (Deut. 6:4-5). For this knowledge the church—and the world—is forever indebted to them.

This knowledge of the one true God was a major factor in Israel's survival in the midst of polytheistic cultures through the centuries. When God called Abraham, he was living in one of the most sophisticated, cosmopolitan, yet pagan cities of that period. Responding to God's call to leave idolatrous Ur and all its false worship and head to a land of promise, Abraham and his family rallied around their faith in the one true God. Israel kept its monotheism during the 400-year sojourn in Egypt, despite the existence of 2,000 various gods. It has been suggested that most of the ten plagues were directed against various Egyptian gods. For example, in the British museum in London a papyrus fragment contains a hymn to the river Nile, lauding it as the indispensable lord and helper of the poor and needy. The first plague turned the river Nile into blood.

Even with the knowledge of the one true God, the Israelites periodically lapsed into idolatry. Soon after their miraculous deliverance from Egyptian bondage, even while

Moses was on Mt. Sinai receiving the Ten Commandments, which specifically forbad the worship of images, the Israelites, in their impatience for Moses' return, begged Aaron to give them a visible god to worship. Yielding to their wish, he molded their golden earrings and jewelry into the shape of a golden calf. As the sun reflected off the shiny gold, Aaron declared, "These are your gods, O Israel, who brought you up out of Egypt" (Ex. 32:4). Then they bowed down, made offerings, and indulged in an orgy of heathen worship. Severe divine punishment followed.

Joshua, in his farewell address to the nation of Israel, reviewed all the wonders God had done through the wilderness wanderings and conquest of Canaan, then challenged them, "Choose for yourselves this day whom you will serve, whether the gods your forefathers served beyond the River, or the gods of the Amorites, in whose land you are living. But as for me and my household, we will serve the Lord" (Josh. 24:15). The people strongly promised to serve the Lord. To their credit, "Israel served the Lord throughout the lifetime of Joshua" (24:31).

But then the Israelites lapsed. "Another generation grew up, who knew neither the Lord nor what he had done for Israel. Then the Israelites did evil in the eyes of the Lord and served the Baals. They forsook the Lord, the God of their fathers, who had brought them out of Egypt. They followed and worshiped various gods of the peoples around them.... In His anger against Israel the Lord handed them over to raiders who plundered them..." (Judges 2:10-14). In distress, they repented. "Then the Lord raised up judges who saved them out of the hands of these raiders" (vs. 16). This entire cycle repeated itself over and over in the days of the judges.

Israel came to its zenith during the reigns of David and Solomon. However, Solomon set the stage for future disaster by intermarriage with women from foreign nations, and maintaining a harem of foreign wives who brought their national gods into his palace. As he "grew old, his wives turned his heart after other gods.... He followed Ashtoreth the goddess of the Sidonians, and Molech the detestable god of the Ammonites" (I Kings 11:4,5). Because of this evil the Lord in anger divided Solomon's kingdom.

Later kings would likewise be guilty of idolatry, which came to its height during the reign of Ahab, whose wife Jezebel reinstituted Baal worship. It was during his reign that the prophet Elijah put to rout 450 prophets of Baal in a contest to ascertain who served the true God. Later kings tolerated the abominable practice of offering their sons and daughters to Molech.

In every generation God had His faithful prophets who showed the absurdity of idolatry. Imagine cutting down a tree, decking it with gold and silver ornaments, fastening it together with hammer and nails so that it wouldn't fall over, and calling it god! Fancy having to prop up a god which can't speak, and which has to be carried because it can't move itself. What a contrast to the Lord God of Israel who is great and mighty (Jer. 10:3-6)!

Despite the warnings of the prophets, the people were married to their idols. Their stiff-necked rebellion culminated in the Assyrian and Babylonian captivities. This produced a permanent cure against any taste for strange gods. Idols were never again openly tolerated in post-exilic Israel.

On a visit to Jerusalem in 1964, my wife and I were looking around a nearly finished museum. A professor of history showed us something an archeologist had just dug up from a heathen Jewish temple. It was an altar with the remains of a sacrifice still on it. The professor told us that this sacrifice came from the first Israelite temple found outside Jerusalem dating back to 800 B.C. He commented that it was fantastic to find a heathen Jewish temple as almost all of them had been destroyed in the revivals, when the zealous removed every vestige of idolatry.

GOD GAVE THE TORAH

Where did the Jews get their aversion to idolatry, and their information about God? Judaism maintains that the Torah, in its narrowest sense the first five books of the Old Testament (Genesis through Deuteronomy), is the primary source of our knowledge of the one true God, although the writings of the prophets are also considered divine revelation. The Torah, God's inspired truth, was revealed to the Israelites from the mouth of God through the hand of Moses.

A synagogue Torah is written on parchment and tied together in a scroll. It's regarded as the holiest ritual object in Judaism and handled with the utmost respect. The Torah contains the Shema, the central affirmation of the Jewish faith, "Hear, O Israel: the Lord our God, the Lord is One." The Shema, a pillar of the synagogue service, is the rallying dogma around which Jews have maintained their identity throughout history. Not only is it among the first words a Jewish child learns to recite, it is also one of the last things a Jew utters before death. Devout Jews faithfully recited the Shema even as they were herded into the gas chambers in the Nazi holocaust, finding strength in the reassurance that somehow behind this seeming insanity existed divine design.

Though the Jews have been a battered people, they have never allowed their belief in the one true God to get strangled by persecution or suffocated by pagan worship.

This self-disclosure of God was never meant to be a unique revelation to Hebrew people alone. God promised to bless Abraham and make him into a great nation, so that in time Israel would be a blessing to all people on earth (Gen. 12:1-3). Israel was not only to be the recipient and custodian of God's special revelation, but also the passage through which the truth of God would bless all nations (Isa. 43:10-12). What helped Israel fulfill its missionary purpose was the Diaspora, the scattering of Jews outside Israel from the time of the Babylonian captivity (597-538 B.C.). Successive dispersions of the Jews among the nations, some voluntary, others forced, spread the knowledge of the one true God among the Gentiles.

SOME TRUTHS ABOUT GOD

British philosopher Herbert Spencer said that God is the unknown and unknowable. Granted, God is unknowable in the sense that it's impossible for mankind to have an exhaustive and complete knowledge of Him. But though we cannot have absolute, full knowledge of God, we can have partial or relative knowledge of an Absolute Being. Since mankind by its own reason cannot discover God, whatever knowledge it may acquire must come because God decides to reveal it. And whatever limited amount He chooses to reveal will be true as well as adequate for the realization of the divine purpose in our lives.

An example of God's self-disclosure is His statement to Moses at the second giving of the Ten Commandments on Mt. Sinai. Passing in front of Moses, He proclaimed, "The Lord, the Lord, the compassionate and gracious God, slow to anger, abounding in love and faithfulness, maintaining love to thousands, and forgiving wickedness, rebellion, and sin. Yet he does not leave the wicked unpunished...." (Ex. 34:6,7).

Using assertions like this along with the entire gamut of Scripture, church theologians through the centuries have attempted to describe the attributes of God, qualities which are in His very nature, and which are demonstrated in His works of creation, providence, and redemption. Of the many fine and various creeds, confessions, and statements of faith, one of the most succinct and encompassing definitions of God is found in the Westminster Shorter Catechism, declaring that God is "a spirit, infinite, eternal, and unchangeable in His being, wisdom, power, holiness, justice, goodness and truth." We follow this order of attributes in giving some thoughts on what God is like.

God is a spirit

God has been defined as Pure Spirit of infinite perfections. He does not have a body. He has neither bulk, form, weight, nor height. He is nonmaterial, not palpable to the senses. He is different from air which has weight and physical substance. He cannot be put in a test tube, nor reduced to a chemical formula.

When Scripture ascribes to God the possession of bodily organs, such as eye, hand, and ear, this is an accommodation of language, termed an anthropomorphism, to help us understand what God is really like—that He can see, do, and hear.

God is invisible

We must not confuse reality with visibility, like the Russian astronaut who boasted on returning to earth, "There is no God. We didn't see any on our flight." Lots of things that are real, like the wind, we cannot see, but they exist nevertheless.

When Scripture speaks of people seeing God, these appearances are but temporary manifestations of God, called theophanies. People were permitted to glimpse a reflection of His glory, but not His essence, for as God told Moses, "No one may see me and live" (Ex. 33:20).

Because God cannot be pictured, the Israelites were not to make any representation of Him, nor to "be enticed into bowing down to them and worshiping things...." (Deut. 4:15-19). Scholars suggest that this prohibition discouraged the development of art in Israel's history. It should be noted

41

that this command does not forbid art, but rather the worship of art objects, for no representation of God can do justice to Him, and only short-circuits true understanding and worship of Him.

God is infinite

God is without limit in His perfections. God's immensity is His infinity related to space. He fills all space. The Psalmist asked, "Where can I flee from your presence?" He declared that wherever he went, God was there (139:7-10).

A little girl returning from Sunday school on a bus sat by a skeptic who, seeing her Sunday school paper, said, "Tell me where God is and I'll give you an apple." The little girl thought a moment, then said, "Sir, tell me a place where God isn't and I'll give you two apples."

God is not confined by space. He can be in two places at one time—a missionary tent with joyous, new believers, and in a western church at worship. He is not diffused through space with one part of Him here and another part there. He is totally in all places at one time, not absent from any part of space. He is present to everything, immanent, yet transcendent. We sometimes call this His omnipresence.

God is eternal

His eternity is His infinity related to time. He is without beginning or end. The Psalmist wrote, "Lord, you have been our dwelling place throughout all generations. Before the mountains were born or you brought forth the earth and the world, from everlasting to everlasting you are God" (90:1,2). He is Alpha and Omega, the first and the last. The same God Who helped Abraham, Moses, Joseph, Gideon and Daniel can be our strength. He is, as the hymn proclaims, "our help in ages past, our hope for years to come."

God is free from succession of time. He is aware of past, present, and future, sees all with one sweep, and knows the end from the beginning. If you were to stand on the main corner of a city and watch a parade go by, you would see the beginning, the middle, and the end, unit by unit, in successive order. But if you were in a low-flying plane, you could survey it all in one view at one moment. A thousand years in His sight are like a day that has just gone by (Ps. 90:4).

God is unchangeable

We live in a world of change. But God is immutable. He said, "I the Lord do not change" (Mal. 3:6). The great I AM is the same yesterday, today, and forever.

The Rock of Ages does not change in His perfections. He cannot change for the worse nor for the better. He is already and always will be perfect. He cannot get stronger or weaker. No deterioration nor improvement is possible. His wisdom never abates. His love is eternal. His mercy is everlasting. His word is forever settled in heaven. His promises are yea and amen.

When the Bible says God repented, the writers are accommodating their language to our limited capacities. If men rebel against Him, His face looks with anger and with threats of judgment on them. But if they repent, His faithful character leads Him to treat them in a new way—with pardon and forgiveness. It is really the sinner who has changed, not God. He ever rewards the good, and punishes the evil. When we walk against the wind, then turn and walk the other way, the wind seems to have changed, but it is we who have made the change.

God is a being

Pantheism says that God is nature and nature is God. But God is separate from, other than, and prior to nature. God existed before the world was created, for He brought it into being. God is not merely the personification of ideals. God possesses self-consciousness and self-determination. He has boundless intelligence, and determines all things after the counsel of His own will. He is angry at sin and punishes the sinner. His names indicate that He is a person.

God is life

Life is a mystery. Life comes from God. He is not merely alive, but the source of all life. A *Reader's Digest* article was titled, "Birth—The Universal Miracle." Though God enabled Abraham and Sarah to become parents in old age, every birth is a miracle. At His word breath departs a body. He raises the dead!

God is independent

The IRS asks us to list our dependents. In reality, all of us are dependent creatures, unable to survive apart from outside help. We call on God for help, but God depends on nobody. He is the only genuinely independent Being, self-existent and self-sufficient. Nothing will happen to Him. "He will not grow tired or weary" (Isa. 40:28). He never suffers a nervous breakdown.

God is wisdom

God knows everything. He is omniscient. He knows all things possible and actual in one eternal act. He knows every star of every constellation by name, the number of hairs on our head, sees every sparrow that falls, and discerns our thoughts.

Creation displays His wisdom. He directs the stars in their clocklike precision. He sends refreshing rain, makes blossoms bud, sustains life, steers the migration of birds. The many wonders of creation were planned by His infinite intelligence.

Providence also reflects His wisdom. His guidance of

our individual lives and history make us cry out, "Oh, the depth of the riches of the wisdom and knowledge of God! How unsearchable his judgments and his paths beyond tracing out!" (Rom. 11:33). He is the only wise God (16:27).

God is power

God is omnipotent. King David extolled the Lord, "...everything in heaven and earth is yours....you are exalted as head over all....you are the ruler of all things" (I Chron. 29:11,12). He is King of kings and Lord of lords.

Earthly kings have been dethroned. But there's one throne that remains and will never be toppled. Time does not affect it, for it is fixed of old. It survives and always will, unshaken and unshattered. Says the Psalmist, "Your throne, O God, will last for ever and ever" (45:6).

God rules in His creation. Can man order the weather? Can man stop a storm and calm the seas? Can he prevent El Niño or a Northeaster? Man is utterly helpless in nature, for it is God who calls the shots.

God is sovereign over the nations. How laughable when men built a tower to try to topple Him from His throne. Dictators may rage and roar, and kings take counsel against Him, but He that sits in the heavens shall laugh and have them in derision, for they cannot take one single step or make one solitary move without His divine permission. The nations are as a drop in the bucket and counted as small dust in the balance. Man rules, but God overrules. The Lord God omnipotent reigns. Once an error was printed on a program of Handel's *Messiah*. Instead of "The Lord God omnipotent reigneth," it said, "resigneth." Never!

God rules in the lives of governments and individuals. When Joseph's brothers begged mercy from him for selling him into slavery, he answered, "Don't be afraid...You intended to harm me, but God intended it for good to accomplish what is now being done, the saving of many lives"

(Gen. 50:19,20). God makes the wrath of men to praise Him. He is sovereign over circumstances.

God is holy

The tales of the gods in pagan polytheism contain vulgar myths and the shameful glorification of sensual desire. What a contrast is the Holy One of Israel!

Holiness is that perfection in virtue of which God eternally wills to maintain His own moral excellence, and to abhor all impurity. God is light, and in Him is no darkness at all. He is free from every stain, and immaculate in every detail. Some theologians consider this His prime attribute. Isaiah refers to Him as the "holy One" over 30 times. He commanded Israel, "Be holy, because I am holy" (Lev. 11:45).

God is just

Because of the revulsion of His holiness against moral impurity, the justice of God requires the infliction of penalties for transgression. But because man is sinful, and God's eyes are too holy to behold evil, God planned a way whereby He could justify the sinner, while still maintaining His own holiness. Justification is the legal act of God whereby on the merits of Jesus' sacrifice on the cross He declares the sinner forgiven and restored to divine favor. Justification is not automatic, but is a gift of God to all who have faith in Christ (Gal. 2:26 and Eph. 2:8-9).

God is good

God's benevolence to all creatures is an evidence of God's love. His goodness is that perfection which prompts Him to deal kindly with all His creatures. He provides food and warm coats for animals. He sustains the sparrow. To humans He gives the pleasures of sight, sound, taste and smell. He shines His sun on the evil and on the good, and sends rain on the gardens of both the believer and the atheist. The bestowal of all good gifts short of salvation has been termed "common grace" and would include the institution of marriage and governmental restraint of evil.

God's "special grace" embraces the attributes involved in the salvation of the saints. Love is that eternal principle of His nature by which He is moved to communicate Himself. Mercy is His compassion exercised towards those in misery or pitiable situations, regardless of their deserts. Grace is His amazing, abounding, unmerited favor to the guilty, granting forgiveness and heaven instead of punishment and perishing. Longsuffering is His patience in postponing judgment on rebellious sinners who repeatedly reject the warnings of His wrath.

God is truth

God is a God of truth, incapable of falsehood and deception. "God is not a man, that he should lie, nor a son of man, that he should change his mind. Does he speak and then not act? Does he promise and not fulfill?" (Num. 23:19). He is utterly reliable. He can be depended upon, does not fail, change, nor disappoint.

People break their word because of shortsightedness, prejudice, or willfulness, but God keeps His pledges. We can live, "standing on the promises which never fail." He is the ground of our confidence, and the guarantor of our hope.

He is faithful in nature. Someone imagined the sun failing to rise one morning. At first people were curious, then frightened, then hysterical. They waited up all the next night, too terrified to sleep. What a relief when the sun came up the second morning. God makes the sun to shine every day.

After the flood God promised, "As long as the earth endures, seedtime and harvest, cold and heat, summer and winter, day and night will never cease" (Gen. 8:22). Regularity in nature is due to the constancy of God, and makes possible the study of science. In fact, some suggest that from the oneness of God flows the concept of a unifying world view in which life is not a hodgepodge of diverse experiences driven by an array of fickle gods, but a universe under the control of an all-powerful God who created and sustains all persons and events in an all encompassing plan.

THE KNOWLEDGE OF GOD
REQUIRES A RESPONSE

Revelation presumes a revealing God, but it also demands a human response. The knowledge of God has ethical implications for mankind. After Moses gave the Ten Commandments to Israel, he proclaimed, "The Lord our God, the Lord is one." He immediately added, "Love the Lord your God with all your heart and with all your soul and with all your strength" (Deut. 6:4,5). God stands in moral relation with mankind, and is the ultimate moral authority. When we respond with obedience, we have fellowship with Him, like Enoch who walked with God, and Abraham who became the friend of God. A person may accept or reject divine wisdom, but for those who obey, "the fear of the Lord is the beginning of knowledge" (Prov. 1:7).

Disraeli, the British Prime Minister during the reign of Queen Victoria, himself a Jew, wrote of the Hebrew nation, "They produced no new order of architecture, in sculpture they did nothing, their religion forbade their making graven images. Their mission was to make known the idea of God as a Being, holy, just and loving."[1]

In Parliament one day a member rose and made disparaging remarks on the Jewishness of Disraeli. Immediately Disraeli drew himself up to his full height, and with much indignation replied, "Sir, you accuse me of being a Jew, and I am proud to answer to the name, and I would remind you that half of Christendom worships a Jew and the other half a Jewess. And I would also remind you that my forefathers were worshiping the one true God while you were naked savages eating acorns in the woods of Britain."[2]

How remarkable that no nation, no intellect, no philosophy, no known history of the world, indicates that any people ever came to the knowledge of the true God apart from His revelation of this truth. Had God not revealed Himself to Israel, Israel would have been idolatrous—and so would those of us today who belong to the church.

Were it not for the Jew, we would be bowing down to gods of wood and stone. But because of the knowledge of the one true God through God's chosen people, Israel, churches have been extolling God's Name continuously for centuries. Last Sunday millions of churchgoers bowed before the Name of God in prayer. And next Sunday that same Name will be lifted up in every part of the globe by worshipers singing the Doxology, praising God from whom all blessings flow. And every Sunday choirs will be singing His Hallelujahs, and congregations will be directing volumes of adoration heavenward, ringing out, "O Lord my God, How Great Thou Art."

NOTES

1. Daniel Fuchs, *How to Reach the Jew for Christ* (Grand Rapids: Zondervan, 1943), p. 19.

2. David Larsen, *Jews*, p. 92.

4

Our Code Of Values

Popular campus speaker Josh McDowell said that in the 1940s the three most common school disciplinary problems were talking in the classroom, chewing gum, and running in the halls. But in the 1980s the statistics indicated that the most common problems were rape, robbery, and assault. In the 90s juvenile violence jumped to a new level—mass shootings and multiple murders on school property by school children during school hours.

Not too many years ago the signboard outside a Michigan high school carried this message, "Have a safe, exciting summer." But in a recent July pranksters broke into the board and rearranged the letters to read, "Have safe sex." After that the board went blank with no message.

Two philosophies are struggling for supremacy in our society. The once prevailing view says that democratic rule depends on people recognizing the existence of God and His system of morals as the glue to hold society together. The other says that people are not confined to any fixed truths or morality, leaving each individual to do whatever he considers right in his own eyes. A few years ago perverse practices were accompanied with guilt and embarrassment, but today are a ticket to appear on TV programs that feature deviant behavior.

A misunderstanding of our nation's Constitution has led

many to believe that religiously based convictions should have no part in public policy. The first two clauses of the First Amendment, "Congress shall make no law respecting an establishment of religion, or prohibiting the free exercise thereof," guarantee religious freedom for all our citizens. It means that the government must not give preference to any one religion or church, and that it not forbid the practice of peoples' beliefs. Erroneously, some have construed the First Amendment to be a wall of separation between church and state. No such wall was ever meant to be, nor was such a separation practiced by those who wrote the Constitution.

The Founding Fathers in their Declaration of Independence stated that all men were created equal, and "endowed by their Creator with certain unalienable Rights." After six months as president, George Washington issued a proclamation for a National Thanksgiving to acknowledge the providence of Almighty God. Every presidential inaugural speech has included a request for divine help. In the dark days of the Civil War in 1863, president Lincoln declared a national day of prayer, "devoutly recognizing the Supreme Authority and just government of Almighty God in all the affairs of men."

The first Congress authorized the appointment of paid chaplains for both the Senate and House. Evidently the men who wrote the First Amendment Religion Clause did not regard paid legislative chaplains and their opening prayers as violating that Amendment. Robert Dugan points out that James Madison, author of the First Amendment, served on the congressional committee of six that recommended the chaplain system.[1]

In 1954 Congress added to the words of the pledge of allegiance the phrase "under God." In 1955 Congress passed a bill to place the inscription "In God We Trust" on all currency and coins. Our leaders certainly did not understand the separation of church and state as excluding religion from the state. The Supreme Court begins each day of oral argument with the bailiff stating, "God save this honorable court." The Founding Fathers wanted the state to be neutral toward religion, but not to restrict nor neutralize religious groups or organizations.

Admittedly the United States is not a Christian nation. However, this country was built on a biblical foundation, its morality based on Judeo-Christian principles. The source of law and justice in our western world has been traced to the Ten Commandments. Howard E. Kershner, former president of the Christian Freedom Foundation and relief administrator who has observed the workings of governments in 40 countries, made this observation. In early British history "...more generally than now, men believed that God created the universe, including man, in accordance with certain very definite principles which have been called the Natural Law or the Moral Law of God. They are well summarized in the Ten Commandments, enlarged by other provisions in the Law of Moses, became the unwritten or Common Law of England....In like manner, the Common Law of Britain was accepted as the basis of our legal system in the United States and in other British colonies...."[2] These Ten Commandments came to us through the Jews.

As you enter the U.S. Supreme Court building, there is, on the right side of the portico, a statue of Moses holding aloft the tablet of the Ten Commandments. Abraham Lincoln once said about the Bible, "...it is the best gift God has given to men.... But for it we could not know right from wrong ."[3]

Harry Truman in his inaugural speech said, "The fundamental basis of this nation's law was given to Moses on the Mount. The fundamental basis of our Bill of Rights comes from the teachings which we get from Exodus and St. Matthew, from Isaiah and St. Paul. I don't think we emphasize that enough these days. If we don't have the proper fundamental moral background, we will finally end up with a totalitarian government which does not believe in rights for anybody except the state."[4]

Those who founded the American system of universal, free public education believed in the indoctrination of students in values which would enable them to become participating members in a democratic republic. The primer in most of these schools was McGuffey's Eclectic Reader, which not only taught three generations to read, but also provided moral instruction on how to live. But through the years the Bible has increasingly been excluded from our public school system, so that today a high court forbids placing the Ten Commandments on the walls of any of our public schools. Interestingly, in 1997 when an Alabama judge was challenged for publicly displaying a wooden plaque of the Ten Commandments on the wall of his courtroom because it purportedly violated the separation of church and state, Congress took an unofficial vote on whether it should be allowed. The nonbinding sense of the Congress resolution in favor of the Decalogue passed, 295-125.

The exclusion of the Ten Commandments from American education has been paralleled by an erosion of morality in American culture. Three-fifths of the senior class at a leading eastern university reportedly lived with a student of the opposite sex without benefit of marriage during a recent academic year. Their defense: "If yours is a meaningful relationship, a marriage license isn't needed."

Recently a TV documentary spent an hour describing the many types of rip-offs in modern dishonest business practices. In his closing remarks the commentator asked, "Who is going to teach ethics to the next generation?"

As part of its message the church and many parents teach the Ten Commandments as furnishing an objective standard of right and wrong—a summary of God's moral law in short propositional statements. Someone commented, "It seems incredible. Man has made 35 million laws and yet hasn't improved on the Ten Commandments."

Many attempts have been made to outline the basic values of life. The ancient Greeks understood the four classic virtues to be fortitude, temperance, prudence, and justice. More recently William Bennett's bestselling *Book of Virtues* recounts a collection of traditional stories that relay ethical principles. But undoubtedly the briefest yet broadest set of moral principles are found in the Ten Commandments. The succinctness of their expression, plus the vast scope of their implications, suggest their divine origin. Only God could have reduced the whole ethical obligation of man to so small a space, and using such pithy pointers.

Thomas Cahill, in his book *The Gifts of the Jews,* suggests that "the originals may actually have been Ten Words—utterly primitive, basic injunctions on the order of 'No-kill,' 'No-steal,' 'No-lie.' These Ten Words (which is the term the Bible uses, not 'Commandments') would have been memorizable by even the simplest nomad, his ten fingers a constant reminder of their centrality in his life."[5]

Cahill goes on to say that there is no document in all the literatures of the world like The Commandments. Though ethical guidelines are found in other cultures, this is the first one offered outside a framework of justification—only God can speak with such authority that no further explanation is needed. These ten words have been received by millions as reasonable and essential, written on the human heart from the beginning of time, needing only to be articulated on Mt. Sinai.

These ten rules cover the entire range of man's duty and forbid every type of wrongdoing. The rest of the Bible is, among other things, a commentary on these ten rules, amplifying, interpreting, warning against their violation, as well as giving historical examples of those who have kept or broken them. For example, David's episode with Bathsheba exemplifies the folly of adultery and the havoc it can wreak within a family. Joseph's resistance to the advances of Potiphar's wife provides a model for abstinence and victory over temptation. Paul wrote that incidents in Israel's history involving punishment for sexual immorality, idolatry, and grumbling, were recorded as warnings to later generations (I Cor. 10:6-11). When one learns the Ten Commandments, he possesses the essence of ethics, the seed-plot of morality, and the kernel of correct conduct.

They were written by the finger of God on two tables of stone (Ex.31:18), inscribed on both front and back sides (32:15). With the mountain smoking and quaking, trumpets blaring and blasting, lightning flashing and thunder crashing, God spoke these ten words (Heb. 12:18-21). This spectacular event dramatized the majesty of the Almighty, the awesome character of the moral law, and the terrifying consequences of its violation. Not surprisingly, the Ten Commandments were placed in the Ark of the Covenant in the Holy of Holies. They were repeated to a new generation of Israelites about to enter the Promised Land after the forty years of wilderness wandering (Deut. 5:1-21). This summary code of values which the church owes to the Jews, expresses God's standard of conduct for people everywhere.

PRINCIPLES OF INTERPRETATION

To correctly understand the full meaning of the Ten Commandments, certain principles of interpretation are helpful.

Rule 1: Prohibitions include opposite positive commands. Positive commands involve contrary negative duties.

A rewrite editor, assigned the task of rewording the Ten Commandments, penned one word, "Don't." However, the eight commandments stated negatively can be rewritten positively—with a "do" or a "shall." For example, "You shall not murder" can be rephrased, "You shall honor the sanctity of human life." Likewise, the two commandments worded positively include the prohibition of contrary behavior. For example, "Honor your father and mother," can be restated, "You shall not disobey your parents."

Rule 2: *Commands extend to thought life.*

Any precept that forbids an outward act also prohibits the inward contemplation of that act. Jesus pointed out that hateful thoughts break the commandment against killing, for they are potential murder. Also, He said that lustful intent breaks the commandment against adultery, for it is mental uncleanness.

Rule 3: *Every inducement which leads to a transgression of a commandment is also forbidden.*

When an act is expressly forbidden, anything that would lead to that act is likewise included in the prohibition. Ezekiel Hopkins, 17th-century Anglican bishop, says that drunkenness, though not specifically mentioned in the Ten Commandments is, in principle, forbidden several times over because it encourages the transgression of several commands. How much easier to steal, lie, or kill, when intoxicated.

Rule 4: *Each command forbids sins of a similar or lesser nature, even while giving the worst violation.*

When the Decalogue says, "You shall not murder," it does not permit half-killing someone, or harming a person in any way. On the contrary, the sixth commandment requires the exercise of every care possible to alleviate the sufferings of humanity.

The command, "You shall not give false testimony," rules

out lying, and related sins like slander, flattery, and exaggeration.

Rule 5: To break one is to be guilty of all.

The commands are so related that to break one is to be under judgment for all. The same authority which forbids murder also forbids lying. To disobey the authority at one point is to defy the authority which stands behind all. "For whoever keeps the whole law and yet stumbles at just one point is guilty of breaking all of it....you have become a lawbreaker" (James 2:10-11).

Rule 6: The Ten Commandments may be summed up under two.

The first four commands relate to our duties toward God; the last six to our duties toward our fellow men. Jesus recognized this twofold division when He answered a lawyer's question as to which is the great commandment in the law (Matt. 22:37-40). Love to God is the first and great commandment, He replied. And the second is like unto it— love to neighbor.

Love to God takes priority over love to man. No one should think that by fulfilling his obligations to his neighbor he has done his complete duty. Unless he has loved God with all his heart, he is guilty of breaking the first and great commandment.

HOW THESE RULES AMPLIFY
THE TEN COMMANDMENTS

Applying these rules of interpretation helps us to a fuller understanding of the Ten Commandments (Ex. 20:3-17).

Commandment 1: "You shall have no other gods before me."

The Ten Commandments begin with God. Since He is

Creator and Sustainer, how natural to make Him our starting point. The first commandment leaves no doubt as to the position God demands in our lives. He will not play second fiddle. Where God is not properly honored, degradation follows. The first chapter of Romans traces the appalling shipwreck in society that results when God does not have first place.

With one deft stroke the first law knocks out several enemies of theism: atheism, polytheism, pantheism, animism, and ignorance. Understanding of God's nature, power, majesty, glory, and grace will give ample reason for bowing in humility and esteeming Him supreme over all.

Commandment 2: *"You shall not make for yourself an idol."*

Some have interpreted this commandment to condemn making or drawing any visible representation. But Solomon's temple, adorned with carved figures of cherubim, palm trees, and open flowers, enjoyed the presence of God, an inexplicable paradox if God were displeased with the making of visible representations.

The art gift comes from God. Man, made in the image of God, has an aesthetic nature which impels him to create and enjoy the beautiful. To make an image is no sin; the iniquity comes from worshiping it. We admire "the ingenuity in making" but decry "the stupidity in worshiping." The command could be restated, "You shall not make anything with the intent to worship it."

Idolatry may be either external or internal. The veneration of visible objects of worship comprises external idolatry. To cherish within our hearts anything that displaces our affection for God constitutes internal idolatry.

A professor in business management at Duke University asked his students to draft a personal strategic plan. With few exceptions, what they wanted fell into three categories: money, power, and things—very big things, includ-

59

ing vacation homes, expensive foreign automobiles, yachts, and even airplanes. Their request of the faculty was, "Teach me to be a money-making machine." These false gods of modern man are as futile and unsatisfying to the spirit as an idol of wood or of stone.

Since negative commands may be stated positively, we could rephrase and amplify the second commandment thus: "Energies should not be expended in the worship of false deities but should be devoted to the service of the true God. We should love God with all our strength."

Commandment 3: *"You shall not misuse the name of the Lord your God."*

The name of God stands for His person and character. This command embodies reverence for God in all deeds and words. Though the avoidance of swearing is not the main thrust, it certainly has reference to that practice. Court oaths are not wrong. Jesus was placed under oath at His trial (Matt. 26:63). It's wrong to implore God's name to some unworthy end, employ it as a gap-filler in conversation.

Swear words are often used in abbreviated form by people who do not realize what oaths they are employing. Professors of languages inform us that "Jehovah" became "by Jove," "God" became "by gad," "Jesus" became "jeeze," "Christ" became "cripes", "jeepers creepers," and "for crying out loud," and "Lord" gave way to "Lawdy" and "law sakes."[6]

Swearing is neither smart, sensible, nor worthwhile. A salesman, asked if he were paid anything for swearing, answered, "No." Came the comment, "You certainly work cheap! You lay aside your character as a gentleman, inflict pain on your friends, break a commandment, and all for nothing!"

We should cultivate a sense of reverence for the name of God. We should also cultivate a sense of God's presence.

It is said that Sir Isaac Newton never mentioned God in conversation without visible pause, and if his head were covered, he would raise his hat. We need to pray often, "Hallowed be Thy name."

Commandment 4: *"Remember the Sabbath day by keeping it holy."*

See chapter 6, "A Day That is Different," for a discussion of this commandment.

The first four commandments give us our duty to God. We should love Him supremely, with our strength, with our speech, and with our time.

Commandment 5: *"Honor your father and your mother."*

This command lays the foundation for family life. Children should respect and obey their parents, not answering impudently, but behaving so as not to bring grief or disgrace on the family name. In later years, they may have an opportunity to repay their parents in some measure for years of loving care.

If parents are to be honored, they must be honorable, worthy of respect and imitation. Parents should provide materially. An old Jewish proverb says, "God couldn't be everywhere so He gave us parents." Parents should provide opportunity for mental development, love unconditionally, and most importantly, nurture their offspring in the admonition of the Lord. Discipline, a good example, and prayer are also needed. In fact, after parents have done their best, prayer may be their only resort as they send their children into a world of devilish pitfalls.

In its broadest sense, the fifth commandment could be stated, "Obey authority." The Puritans often expanded this command to include other authority relationships, like employers and government rulers. If a child learns to respect his parents, he will more readily honor his teachers, obey the laws of the land, defer to his employer, and obey the Bible.

Commandment 6: *"You shall not murder."*

Murder is the willful, unauthorized taking of human life. The Old Testament made a distinction between accidental and willful killing. Cities of refuge were provided as sanctuary for those who killed unintentionally. Though verses like Gen. 9:6 teach capital punishment, it should only be practiced when guilt has been established beyond the slightest doubt, and only then in the absence of mitigating factors. To avoid the possibility of executing an innocent person some evangelicals hold that the most severe penalty should be life without possibility of parole.

Forbidden would be suicide, mercy-killing, and abortion except in the case of rape, incest, or the safety of the mother. Half-killing someone is forbidden. Knifing, shooting, striking, bombing, and all acts of bodily assault are proscribed. Any deed which tends to injure, maim, or shorten human life is included in this commandment.

In its positive aspect this command supports the sanctity of life, the care of health through doctors, nurses, hospitals, medicine, sanitary measures, and non-pollution. In reality, murder begins in the heart with envy, hate, prejudice or anger. The place to get victory is in the beginning stage where murder is still embryonic. Then anger cannot hatch into vindictive speech or fatal act.

Commandment 7: *"You shall not commit adultery."*

God invented sex. Prudish concepts of sex as sordid and sinful receive no support in Scripture. The Bible says that marriage is honorable. However, sex is ordained of God to occur within the context of marriage for companionship and procreation. Dallas Cowboy star Roger Staubach was once blindsided by a reporter who asked him how he felt when comparing himself with another well-known quarterback who was sexually active and always pictured with a different woman on his arm. Roger replied, "I'm sure I'm just as sexually active as he. The difference is that mine is with one woman."

The Westminster Larger Catechism gives a comprehensive catalogue of prohibited sexual behaviors including, "adultery, fornication, rape, incest, sodomy, and all unnatural lusts; all unclean imaginations, thoughts, purposes, and affections."

Homosexuality and same-sex marriage are not natural ways of life. God's plan does not involve the union of two men, nor of two women, but one male and one female, just as He joined them at the beginning.

Retired Bethel College professor and Old Testament scholar Arthur Lewis says, "In every case where the law of chastity is violated in the Old Testament, evil and violent consequences result. We have, therefore, from the Hebrew Bible, not only the counsel of wise teachers in Israel and the guidance of the Torah from Moses, but the consistent evidence of history and human experience in support of sexual purity and abstinence outside marriage."[7]

Commandment 8: "You shall not steal."

This command assumes the right of private ownership. Obviously bank robberies, street muggings, and house burglaries are forbidden, but some who never overtly or forcibly take another's property find it easy to rob impersonal organizations, "who would never miss the little we take." The manager of an aircraft company ordered workers to assemble in the yard for a group photo, but the guilt-ridden workers thought it to be an inspection. Suddenly the ground was littered with quickly abandoned tools and equipment they had hidden in their lockers.

Insurance companies are bilked out of millions in false

claims. Academic cheating is widespread. Income tax evasion is common. Employees get away with shoddy work. Business hides its share of questionable practices.

Stewardship is the antithesis of stealing. The positive implications of the eighth commandment are found in this biblical advice, "He who has been stealing must steal no longer, but must work, doing something useful with his own hands, that he may have something to share with those in need" (Eph. 4:28). Obedience to this precept requires honesty, industry, and generosity.

Commandment 9: *"You shall not give false testimony."*

Lying is asserting that which is not true with intent to deceive. Kidding is not lying, nor is an honest mistake in a statement, nor a work of fiction, nor the use of figurative language, nor a change of viewpoint, nor concealing part of the truth when it's not necessary to tell everything.

One can lie in many ways: perjury, half-truth, quoting out of context, pretending, slander, detraction, mock self detraction, boasting, flattery, exaggeration.

Lying affects the liar, sabotaging one's integrity and self-respect, and eventually catches up with us.

Lying affects others. It disrupts the fabric of society which operates on a supposed foundation of truth, fracturing relationships with family, friends, and business associates. Too often international pacts prove nothing but scraps of paper.

Lying affects our relationship with God. Lying is contradictory to His nature, for He is truth. We must learn to keep our promises, fulfill our contracts, and "put off falsehood and speak truthfully" to each other (Eph. 4:25).

Commandment 10: *"You shall not covet."*

Covetousness is excessive desire for what one does not have, especially what belongs to another. Compared to the other commandments which involve overt transgressions like murder and theft, this one sounds quite harmless. One clergyman said that in all his prayer meetings and counseling sessions he had never once heard the sin of covetousness confessed. But far from an inconsequential infraction, this commandment is pivotal because it involves a sin which breeds other sins. For example, coveting a man's wife may lead to adultery; coveting his valuables may lead to stealing, even murder. Biblical writers list it among the most flagrant of sins (Eph. 5:3-5).

This command indicates its divine origin, for only God knows what goes on in the human mind. No police radar can detect covetousness. But the secrets of our heart are open before God.

To overcome covetousness we must check the first inner motions toward any sinful desire. Says Proverbs, "Guard your heart, for it is the wellspring of life" (4:23). We should cultivate contentment. A frugal farmer, visiting a new shopping center, exclaimed, "I've never seen so many things I can do without." We must practice tithing and generous giving.

WHY GOD GAVE US THIS SUMMARY
OF MORALITY

One reason God gave the Decalogue was to show us how far short of His standard of perfection we have fallen, silencing every mouth and rendering the whole world guilty before God. Through the law we become conscious of sin (Rom. 3:20), and are convicted of our need for forgiveness.

The law serves as a deterrent to sin. As Dr. Carl Henry said, "Even where there is no saving faith, the Law serves to restrain sin and to preserve the order of creation by proclaiming the will of God....It has the role of a magistrate who is a terror to evildoers."[8]

Our children need to be grounded in the meaning and ramifications of the Ten Commandments. Untold suffering, trouble, and sorrow might be averted. Princeton criminologist John DiIulio Jr. believes that the big curse of life in the inner city is growing up without loving, capable, reponsible adults who teach you right from wrong."[9]

Also, God gave us the Ten Commandments to provide a road map to happiness. Some people speak about the oppressive nature of the prohibitions in the Decalogue. They consider their negativism a joyless enemy and a horrible burden in life. But God gave them because He loves us, not because He wants to hamper our fun. To disobey the commandments leads to loss of joy, a guilty conscience, often to jail, and sometimes to the psychiatrist's office. Dr. Sydney Sharman supports the thesis that a life-style based on the Decalogue reduces immeasurably the vulnerability of an individual to neurotic ill health. Using several case histories, the psychiatrist illustrates how the Decalogue offers not only a basis of prevention, but also a cure for many modern neuroses.[10]

Dr. Cyrus Gordon, Hebrew scholar and professor of Near Eastern Studies at Brandeis University, said, "The Ten Commandments are a landmark in human history, because they sum up in a few verses so much of what society and the individual need for a good, orderly, and productive life. If we were to follow these sacred precepts, we would become as free as possible from the turmoil that results from transgression, and from the dissatisfaction that stems from coveting. We would have a more stable society in which parents and children would be better united in respect and love. We would be more attune to the divine order of things through following the commandments of God."[11]

Just as following a book of directions will help us operate an appliance at its best, so following the divine code of ethical directions help humans achieve maximum satisfaction in life situations. After giving the Ten Commandments the Lord added, "Oh, that their hearts would...keep all my commands always, so that it might go well with them and their children forever!" (Deut. 5:29).

Here's a recent letter to the editor of our local, Rockland County (NY) newspaper, "In traditional Judaism a man celebrates his second mitzvah 70 years after he has celebrated his first, at age 13. I have just gone through this ceremony again, at age 83, and was grateful for what it refreshed in my memory about my religion. Most particularly, I appreciated more than ever the treasury of wisdom and many fundamental teachings that my people gave to the world and that the other religions have borrowed from.

"For my second celebration the weekly Torah portion was Deuteronomy, and I suddenly realized that the recent noise... about 'family values' was artificial, contrived and hollow. We Hebrews had written about it 3,000 years ago.

"What is a more fundamental family value than 'honor thy father and thy mother.' And why isn't the commandment that 'thou shalt not commit adultery' the greatest underpinning to family stability. Or why isn't it basic to family values that 'thou shalt not bear false witness against thy neighbor,' nor 'covet thy neighbor's wife' or 'thy neighbor's house, his field, ..or anything that is thy neighbor's?'

"And where is there greater family value than in an environment where family members do not steal and do not murder?

"Come off it ...go back to Deuteronomy 5 of the Hebrew Bible, and let's all get under the umbrella of its teachings for common wisdom and guidance."[12]

In modern parlance the Decalogue says, "Do not smash up another person's family life. Respect his and her life, marriage, property and reputation."

A writer for the Wall St. Journal, Dennis Prager, asserted, "Though I am a Jew, I believe that a vibrant Christianity is essential if America's moral decline is to be reversed. And despite theological differences, Christianity and Judaism have served as the bedrock of American civilization."[13] Yes, this code of values, which is central to the church's moral teaching, and which has provided the basis for our most treasured national values, is rooted in Old Testament Judaism, another major debt the church owes the Jews.

NOTES

1. Robert Dugan, *Stand and Be Counted* (Sisters, Oregon: Multnomah Books, 1995), p. 202.

2. "The Source of Law and Justice," *Applied Christianity*, July 1972, p. 2.

3. *Abraham Lincoln: Wisdom & Wit*, ed. Louise Bachelder (White Plains, New York: Peter Pauper Press, 1965), p. 12.

4. Quoted in Robert Dugan, p. 199.

5. Thomas Cahill, *The Gifts of the Jews* (New York: Doubleday, 1998), p. 139.

6. Lawrence E. Nelson, *Roving Bible*, pp. 128-129.

7. *Biblical Reflections*, Summer 1995, No. 8, p.3.

8. Carl F. Henry, *Christian Personal Ethics* (Grand Rapids: Wm. B. Eerdmans Publishing Co., 1957), p. 355.

9. *Newsweek*, April 6, 1998, p. 25.

10. Dr. Sydney Sharman, *Psychiatry, the Ten Commandments, and You* (New York: Dodd, Mead, and Company, n.d.).

11. The Ten Commandments, *Christianity Today*, April 10, 1964, pp. 3-6.

12. Max Mason in the *Rockland Journal News*, West Nyack, New York, August 30, 1995.

13. *Wall Street Journal*, December 15, 1997, p. A-22.

5

Founders Of
The Church

Back in the 80s a caller from the Billy Graham organization asked me to contact a Jewish gentleman living in the next town who had asked for information on the Christian faith. When I introduced myself by phone as a Baptist minister, he wanted nothing to do with me. Before he could hang up I mentioned that I knew some Jewish believers. Immediately his interest perked.

It so happened that our next Sunday night service had a round table discussion, involving twelve Jewish Christians. Herb Bluttman came to the service, where some Jewish Christians led him to acknowledge Jesus as his Messiah. He attended our church regularly, was baptized, became a member, and grew remarkably in biblical knowledge. After six years he informed me that he somehow didn't feel at home in our church. I understood, replying that I wouldn't feel at home in a synagogue. He joined a Messianic group in the next town along with his wife, Ruth, who also became a believer, and supported that ministry for several years. We keep in touch and often dine together.

Messianic Judaism is a term of recent usage. Yet, in reality, the first church was a Messianic church. The church made its debut, not in a Gentile city, but in Jerusalem, the very capital and center of Judaism. It was there that the gospel, which is about a Jew, was first preached by Jews to Jews. And for the first several years virtually every member of the church was a Jew. Thus, another debt we owe the Jew is the church—its very origin and existence. That's why many tourists to the Holy Land count it a highlight to worship in one of Jerusalem's few small Messianic congregations and experience the blessing of attending a service in the city where the church began.

Today when we think of a church, we picture a sanctuary full of Gentiles—with no Jewish members. But in the early church it was just the reverse; the membership was exclusively Jewish—no Gentiles. And when Gentiles did begin to accept Jesus as their Savior, some Jewish leaders objected to welcoming the Gentiles unless they first submitted to Jewish law. (Luke shares these stories throughout Acts.)

JEWS FOR JESUS RALLY

Seven weeks after Jesus' crucifixion and resurrection a marvelous event occurred in Jerusalem. Moishe Rosen calls it "the first ever Jews for Jesus Witnessing Campaign." Gathered in the Upper Room were 120 disciples—all Jews. The Holy Spirit came upon them with great power so that they began to speak in other languages. Going outdoors into the streets, they told everyone about Jesus, their Savior and Lord. Present at Jerusalem for the Feast of Pentecost were Jews and proselytes from "every nation under heaven" (Acts 2:5). Amazed at hearing the gospel in their native tongues, they listened to Peter who used the phenomenon as a springboard to preach the gospel. Three thousand were saved that day (2:41). Excitement over their newly found Messiah was so contagious that many more heard their testimony and believed. "The Lord added to their number daily those who were being saved" (2:47). Just Jews.

Led by Peter and John, the disciples continued their ministry, filling Jerusalem with their Spirit-powered preaching. The number of believers swelled to about five thousand (4:4). All Jews. Though the religious establishment tried to stop these Jewish missionaries by flogging them, the disciples rejoiced that they could suffer for Jesus' sake and kept on witnessing (5:40,41).

People sometimes ask, "If Jesus is the Messiah, why haven't the rabbis believed?" A good response is that in the very early days of the church a substantial group of religious leaders did come to faith. After the appointment of seven deacons to handle the daily distribution of food to the poor saints, "the number of disciples in Jerusalem increased rapidly, and a large number of priests became obedient to the faith" (6:7). Perhaps some of these priests had witnessed the ripping of the curtain in front of the Holy of Holies at the precise hour on the day Jesus died (Matt. 27:51). The tearing, from top to bottom, indicated on later reflection that a divine hand had been responsible, thus helping to verify the claims of Jesus of Nazareth .

It always amazes me to hear someone assert that a Jew cannot be a Christian. Or that a Jew who accepts Jesus as His Messiah ceases to be a Jew. Or that the notion of Hebrew Christianity is a theological impossibility. The simple truth is that Peter, James, John, the rest of the Twelve, and all these early Jewish believers were Christians. They didn't renounce their Jewish heritage, and were not considered to have done so. The apostle Paul proudly declared his Jewishness (Rom. 11:1; 2 Cor. 11:22), and said concerning himself that he was "circumcised on the eighth day, of the people of Israel, of the tribe of Benjamin, a Hebrew of Hebrews" (Phil. 3:5).

There are Gentile Christians and there are Jewish Christians, the latter often called Messianic Jews today. Less than 30 years after Pentecost on a visit to Jerusalem, Paul was told by the elders of the Jerusalem church, "how many thousands of Jews have believed" (Acts. 21:20). The word for "thousands" gives us our English "myriads" and means an innumerable multitude. The Twentieth Century New Testament translates the above verse, "That the Jews which have become believers in Christ may be numbered by tens of thousands."

Many Christian Jews today refer to themselves as completed or fulfilled Jews.

CONVERSION OF GENTILES

Though Jesus had commanded His disciples to witness for Him beyond Jerusalem to Judea, Samaria, and to the end of the earth (1:8), the gospel did not immediately move beyond Jerusalem, not till the death of Stephen disturbed the peace of the church.

Samaria

At the stoning of Stephen, a great persecution erupted against the church at Jerusalem. Except for the apostles all the believers were scattered throughout Judea and Samaria. Philip, a deacon, proclaimed Christ in Samaria with the result that many believed and were baptized.

Still the Jewish believers showed no inclination to preach the gospel to the Gentiles. How would the Lord overcome their provincialism and help them reach out beyond the confines of their own nation? He chose Peter, who had opened the door to the Jews to also open the door to the Gentiles. But the Lord had to prepare Peter for this assignment.

Cornelius

Gentile Cornelius, a godly Roman centurion in Caesarea, was told in a vision to send for Peter in Joppa. When the centurion's messengers were about to arrive in Joppa, Peter, praying on the roof, had a vision of a sheet descending from heaven containing unclean food. Told to eat, Peter protested that he had never eaten anything non-kosher. A divine voice answered, "Do not call anything impure that God has made clean" (10:15). To make sure Peter got the message, the Lord repeated it twice more. As Peter puzzled over the meaning of the vision, the Gentile messengers arrived at the door.

The significance of it all dawned on Peter—the Gentiles who turn to the Messiah of Israel are not to be considered unclean. Peter accompanied the messengers back to the home of Cornelius where, while Peter was preaching, the Spirit fell upon the listeners. The Jewish believers who had come with Peter were amazed that the gift of the Holy Spirit had been poured out "even on the Gentiles" (10:45). Peter baptized them immediately.

When this news reached the apostles, Peter was called on the carpet because of his association with Gentiles. Peter recounted the episode from start to finish, ending, "Who was I to think that I could oppose God?" His explanation silenced them. Instead, the leaders praised God, "So then, God has granted even the Gentiles repentance unto life" (11:18).

Antioch

Peter's experience prepared the Jerusalem leadership for a situation that developed at Antioch. At first those scattered at Stephen's persecution told the gospel "only to Jews" (11:19). But some began to speak the message to Gentiles so that a great number in Antioch turned to the Lord. When news of this reached Jerusalem, the leaders sent Barnabas to investigate. Convinced that the Lord's hand was upon the movement, Barnabas joyfully encouraged the Gentile converts to remain true to the Lord (11:20-26).

Needing help in the growing ministry, Barnabas sought out Paul in Tarsus, and brought him to Antioch. Barnabas knew of Paul's remarkable conversion, and of his teaching potential for the edification of the new believers. For a year Barnabas and Paul taught great numbers of people. Then the church at Antioch set apart Barnabas and Paul for a missionary assignment.

TO THE JEW FIRST

Though at his conversion Paul was informed by the Lord that he would be sent "far away to the Gentiles" (22:21), Paul made it his practice to go to the Jews first. For example, on their first missionary journey Paul and Barnabas, arriving in Salamis, proclaimed the word in Jewish synagogues (13:5).

Paul knew that in the fullness of time—at the correct point in history—God sent down His Son to earth. Paul was aware that the Jewish population was ripe for the Messiah's coming. The following factors helped shape and sharpen Paul's policy of evangelizing Jews first:

Scattering

Through the Assyrian and Babylonian captivities, Jews had been dispersed among many nations. Also, many Jews had voluntarily migrated to new countries in pursuit of trade. This scattering was known as the Diaspora. A list of the countries represented at Pentecost shows how widely Jews had spread (2:5-11).

Scripture

Wherever they went the Jews carried the Old Testament and their monotheism. Their lofty concept of worship of the one true God exercised a strong persuasion in the cultures in which they settled. Long available for all Greek-speaking people, which would include almost all in the Roman Empire, was the Septuagint translation of the Old Testament.

Sabbath

Scattered Jews did not lose their identity, but maintained their faith by meeting regularly on the Sabbath. Week after week they were reminded of their Messianic hope.

Synagogue

Their meeting-place was the synagogue. Every town with enough Jews had at least one synagogue. If males numbered less than ten, they would meet by a river, as at Philippi where Paul found the merchant Lydia and others worshiping (16:13).

Their services included prayers, Psalm-singing, Scripture reading, and an exhortation based on the Scripture, elements copied in the early church and found in our services today. A visiting teacher might be invited to give the exposition. This explains how Jesus was invited to speak in various synagogues, including the one in his hometown of Nazareth (Lk. 4:15-27). The disciples took advantage of this practice in those early decades before the doors of the synagogue were closed to them.

Strangers

The synagogue attracted many Gentiles who felt a need of spiritual help. Philosophy had reached its zenith a few centuries before with the thinking of Plato and Aristotle, and had degenerated into various schools of thought, mostly fatalistic, atheistic, materialistic, and purposeless. The Greek gods were cruel, deceitful, and immoral. The mystery cults were unable to quench widespread thirst for cleansing and security.

Because of the failure of their philosophy and religions,

Gentiles attended the synagogue services, some of them becoming full-fledged proselytes—Gentiles converted to Judaism and duly circumcised. Devout worshipers who remained uncircumcised were called God-fearers. A Roman military officer who built a synagogue at Capernaum, and the Roman centurion Cornelius, are examples of God-fearing Gentiles.

Savior

The Old Testament predicted a coming Messiah. Scholars list dozens of Messianic prophecies. With the Jews and their Scriptures scattered so widely, people in widespread places would have some idea of a coming Messiah. Messianic expectation helps explain why three wise men from the east, apparently non-Jews, followed a star in search of the newborn King of the Jews.

What a mission field these factors prepared for Paul! Wherever he went all over the known world were multitudes of Jews, conversant with their Scriptures, possessing the hope of a coming Messiah, meeting regularly every Sabbath to hear these same Scriptures expounded, joined by proselytes and God-fearers who shared the same anticipation. Paul's typical strategy on entering a new town or city is recorded in Acts 17:1-4, "When they had passed through Amphipolis and Apollonia (apparently no synagogues in those towns), they came to Thessalonica, where there was a Jewish synagogue. As his custom was, Paul went into the synagogue, and on three Sabbath days he reasoned with them from the Scriptures, explaining and proving that the Christ had to suffer and rise from the dead. 'This Jesus I am proclaiming to you is the Christ,' he said. Some of the Jews were persuaded and joined Paul and Silas, as did a large number of God-fearing Greeks and not a few prominent women." The promises of the Old Testament had been fulfilled in Jesus of Nazareth!

Paul's practice was to take the gospel to the Jew first, as He wrote to the Romans, "I am not ashamed of the gospel, because it is the power of God for the salvation of everyone who believes, first for the Jew, then for the Gentile" (1:16).

Because of a general peace enforced by Roman rule, Paul was able to travel with comparative ease over safe seas and fast roads which fanned out in network fashion to access the synagogues of the empire. Yet as more and more Gentiles accepted Christ as Savior and Lord in the first two decades of the church, a major problem arose among Jewish Christians: *Must Gentiles become Jews in order to become Christians?*

Today when so many churches are 100% Gentile, or almost so, it seems strange to recall that in the first few years of church history, congregations were nearly 100% Jewish. Moreover, some Jewish leaders did not wish to allow Gentile believers into their churches, insisting they first submit to Jewish law. This was the question that precipitated the first church council—can a Gentile be accepted into the church without first becoming a Jew?

The controversy began when Judaizing teachers from Jerusalem arrived in Antioch and insisted on Gentile male converts submitting to the Jewish rite of circumcision in order to be saved. When Paul and Barnabas returned from their first missionary journey, they strenuously resisted this heresy (15:1,2).

The issue was critical. Either a person was saved by faith alone, or by faith plus works or ceremonies. If the latter, then the gospel of grace was essentially revoked. Paul and Barnabas recognized this as not only a battle for Christian liberty, but also a struggle over the very nature of the gospel. They had seen countless Gentiles won to Christ apart from Mosaic lawkeeping. With the missionary movement expected to penetrate more deeply into Gentile territory, this question would have to be settled.

Unable to silence the Judaizers from Jerusalem, the church at Antioch appointed Paul and Barnabas along with others to consult with the leaders at Jerusalem on this dispute. The council rendered a decisive verdict in favor of salvation apart from circumcision and Jewish law, even though the very core of the early church was Jewish. Gentiles who today enjoy the fellowship of a church should remember their Jewish legacy.

The gospel was first spread by Jews. The first gospel literature, the New Testament books, were penned almost exclusively by Jews. Paul, usually considered the most effective missionary of all times, was Jewish and carried the gospel to the Mediterranean world. Tradition says that when the apostles grasped the meaning of the Great Commission, they decided on a strategy of missions by dividing the known world into zones of responsibility among themselves. Then each traveled his separate way, together covering most points of the compass. One tradition has Peter in Rome; John in Ephesus; Andrew in Greece; Philip in Asia Minor; Bartholomew in Armenia; Matthew in Ethiopia; Thaddaeus in Mesopotamia; Simon the Zealot in the Persian Gulf; and Thomas in India. The missionary movement began with Jews. If it were possible to trace our spiritual lineage to its source, most of us would discover that we owe our salvation ultimately to a Jewish missionary. Jews carried the light to the Gentiles. And many gave their lives in doing so.

BREAKDOWN OF JEWISH-CHRISTIAN RELATIONSHIP

According to Daniel Juster, after the death of the apostles, the control of the church passed into the hands of leaders, many of whom were non-Jewish and unappreciative of their Jewish heritage. To some the destruction of Jerusalem in A.D. 70 indicated God's ultimate rejection of

Israel. Others could not understand Jews continuing Old Testament practices. Barnabas (A.D. 100) spoke disparagingly of the Jews, making any effective contact with the synagogue impossible. Ignatius of Antioch (early 2nd century) spoke of the "uselessness of all things Jewish."[1]

The gap widened between church and synagogue. The church considered itself the true Israel, and regarded Old Israel as reprehensible before God. Bishop Ambrose (4th century) said that synagogue-burning was not a sin. Augustine (also 4th century) spiritualized the promises to Israel to mean the triumph of the church. Chrysostom (also 4th century) preached eight sermons against the Jews. As the renowned Patriarch of Constantinople, his viewpoint influenced the attitude of organized Christianity.

After Christianity became the state religion in the 4th century, the church became Gentilized. A Jew who wanted to accept the Jewish Messiah had to renounce everything Jewish including "all customs, rites, legalisms, unleavened breads and sacrifices of lambs of the Hebrews, sacrifices, prayers, aspersions, purifications, sanctifications and propitiations, fasts, and new moons and Sabbaths, and superstitions, and hymns and chants and observances and synagogues, and the food and drink of the Hebrews;...every law, rite and custom."[2] Jews were commonly called "Christ-killers." Luther's sermons against the Jews were recounted centuries later by Nazi leaders in defense of their notorious actions in the Holocaust. Other glaring examples of torture and devastation of the Jews were the Inquisition in 16th century Spain and the 19th century pogroms in Russia.

From the 5th to the 18th century the church had no room for congregations of Messianic Jews. Messianic Jewish history ceased to be communal but became the stories of individual believers. Every generation had its share of Jewish converts. Thousands of Jews were received into church membership in the 19th century, including such notables as

Disraeli, prime minister of Great Britain, Neander, professor of Ecclesiastical History in Berlin: and Alfred Edersheim, lecturer at Oxford. Harold A. Sevener, in his book *A Rabbi's Vision*, a 673-page centennial history of Chosen People Ministries, says, "During the latter half of the nineteenth century, over twenty-nine Jewish missions, or organized evangelistic outreaches to the Jewish people, were established."[3]

The Joseph Rabinowitz story

A scholarly study records the establishment of a Messianic congregation in Kishineff, the capital of the province of Bessarabia in southwestern Russia in 1885. On a visit to Palestine, Joseph Rabinowitz, a prominent and popular lawyer, deeply concerned for the welfare of his Jewish brethren, came from his study of Scripture to a thoroughly evangelical creed. Turned down by the Russian Orthodox authorities to form a Hebrew-Christian church, he was able to secure permission to convene meetings under the banner of "Israelites of the New Covenant." He is considered the founder of the first truly Hebrew Christian Messianic Jewish community without the outside direction of Gentile churches or missions. His was the only synagogue in Russia where, every Sabbath, Jewish services were held in Jesus' name, and the gospel was preached to Jews in the Jewish language to audiences from 50 to 200. After his death the work faltered because of the massive killing of Jews in 1903.[4]

TODAY'S MESSIANIC JEWISH MOVEMENT

Regarding a recent movement of Messianic Jews, Arthur F. Glasser comments: "During the last 20 years a movement has been gathering momentum throughout the world, indeed wherever there are Jewish communities. Not only has the older pattern continued of individual Jews here and there coming to faith in Jesus and assimilating into Gentile churches.... But something new, though with an ancient history, is increasingly emerging in our day—the resurgence of 1st century distinctly Messianic Jewish congregations. Their members are possessed by a commitment to their Jewish heritage and the determination to meet together and utilize a characteristically Jewish worship style that missiologists cannot but comment."[5]

The term, "Messianic Judaism," seems to have come into common use in the 1960s, when Jewish Christian congregations sprang up everywhere. The organization of various unions of Messianic Jewish Congregations has given wider circulation to the term. Daniel Juster points out that "Messianic Judaism is not a completely new movement, but rather the resurrection of a very old movement."[6] The terms "Hebrew Christian" and "Messianic Jew" are really synonymous—Jewish believers in Christ. Messianic Judaism refers to Jews who follow Jesus, are loyal to Jewish heritage, and have concern for evangelizing Jews.

Can a Messianic believer retain a Jewish way of life?

First reaction of many Gentile Christians on hearing of Jewish Christians observing some of their holidays and feasts is: Aren't we now in the New Testament era, and haven't all Old Testament practices been abolished? The first time a Jewish mission asked if they could sponsor a Passover Seder in our church, my initial thought was: Didn't Jesus, our Passover, fulfill that Old Testament festival? Over 250 people attended, including 57 Jewish neighbors, all hearing a clear explanation of how the various elements of the Passover point to Jesus Christ.

Paul certainly kept some Old Testament practices after his conversion. On his final visit to Jerusalem, he expressed his intent to join four men in a vow of purification. The church elders were delighted, saying, "You see, brother, how many thousands of Jews have believed, and all of them are

81

zealous for the law. They have been informed that you teach all the Jews who live among the Gentiles to turn away from Moses, telling them not to circumcise their children or live according to our customs ....The next day Paul took the men and purified himself along with them. Then he went to the temple to give notice of the date when the days of purification would end and the offering would be made for each of them" (Acts 21:20-26).

Some Bible teachers claim that Paul was wrong to observe this Old Testament practice since salvation supposedly did away with the law. But Charles R. Erdman, in his exposition of Acts, disagrees. "This, however, is quite to miss the point of the story and to misunderstand the principles of Paul. He had rejected the Law as a means of justification, not as a mode of life; he did not trust to its observance to secure his salvation, but he practiced its ceremonies as one who loved his nation and who was glad to avoid any needless offense to his fellow countrymen."[7] He wrote, "To the Jews I became like a Jew, to win the Jews....I have become all things to all men so that by all possible means I might save some" (I Cor. 9:19-23).

By allowing its people to retain their Jewish customs, Messianic faith becomes more winsome and less offensive. It provides a forceful demonstration that Jewish believers have not forsaken their Jewishness. Such a congregation furnishes a comfortable environment for its members to appreciate their Jewish roots and to ease tension between their Jewish identity and New Testament Christianity. Such fellowships also create a supportive atmosphere in which to raise children, e.g. sponsoring bar-mitzvah ceremonies. In addition, the presence of Gentile members, which is true in most Messianic groups, testifies that both Jew and Gentile are in fact one in Christ, the middle wall of partition broken down.

Jewish believers can retain their own culture just as

Gentile believers can retain theirs. A Jewish Christian and his wife were talking with the pastor of a large church about a mutual acquaintance, an ardent Jewish worker. The pastor remarked, "I really appreciate his ministry but I must ask, Why does he have to act so Jewish?" The Jewish Christian was dumbfounded, but his wife recovered quickly and asked, "Why do you have to act so Gentile?" The Gospel is not chained to any particular culture. Gentiles are not expected to change cultures at conversion. Neither does a Jew need to stop being Jewish when he believes in the Jewish Messiah, specially since the Gospel was Jewish to begin with.

All Old Testament customs maintained, however, should be consistent with New Testament teaching. Many practices would be optional such as dietary rules, and not be forced on others. The observance of Old Testament feasts would focus on the centrality of Jesus' sacrifice. The theme of the Epistle to the Hebrews is the superiority of Christ to the Old Testament priesthood and sacrificial system with His final, sufficient, once-for-all death on the cross, so animal sacrifices are annulled. Some Messianic congregations prefer to meet on the Jewish Sabbath. More than once have I spoken at Messianic weekly services that met on Friday night or Saturday.

How many Messianic Christians?

David Stern says that precise numbers of Messianic Jews are hard to come by because believers are hard to define and to locate. Estimates range from 50,000 to 100,000 congregants meeting in Messianic groups in the USA; a late figure goes as high as 150,000. In Israel, the number is somewhere around 5,000 in about 50 congregations which is about 3/20th of 1% of a Jewish population nearing four million. In Great Britain 3,000 to 5,000. In western Europe, less than 1%. In Russia, tens of thousands. More than 120

Messianic congregations may be found in the USA, with the total constantly rising. Many Jewish believers attend predominantly Gentile churches; others are virtually isolated.[8]

It was my practice on Tuesday evenings to visit the homes of those who had visited our church for the first time the previous Sunday. One September night in the 70s, I called at an apartment door which bore the sign, "Abe Rothberg—Tailor." Abe, whom I had never met, greeted me cordially, and called his wife, who had attended the previous Sunday. She, in turn, greeted me warmly. They were Jewish, and their only son, Stuart, in his 20s, was in the army in Omaha, Nebraska. Stuart had tried everything to find the answer to life, but the search had been in vain until a fellow soldier led him to faith in Jesus. The previous Christmas Stuart came home and told his parents. Said his mother, "Most Jewish mothers would have thrown him out, but he led Abe and me to Jesus."

The Sunday before Christmas I Invited Stuart to give his testimony after our choir's presentation of *The Messiah*. Stuart told his story in a most articulate, winsome way. His parents were both baptized not long before his father's death. His mother, who memorized over sixty Bible verses while in her 60s, continues faithfully to this day, often praying aloud in a church service to the God of Abraham, Isaac, and Jacob.

After Stuart's discharge from the army, he graduated from Trinity Seminary in Deerfield, IL, working for a while with Jews for Jesus in Chicago. For a few years he served as pastor of the Olive Tree Congregation in the Chicago area, a church formed back in 1979 as a place where both Jewish and Gentile believers could feel comfortable worshiping together. Similar congregations have started in other places, using the same name. Today married and the father of three boys, he is the teaching pastor of a thriving Texas church. The name "Olive Tree" comes from Paul's analogy in Romans 11:16-27, where he likens Israel to an olive tree, and Gentiles to wild branches grafted into the olive tree. The name seems fitting for Messianic congregations where a substantial number of Gentiles also worship.

Grafted-in Gentiles owe a debt to the original root from which they derive their support. The New Testament, as many Jews have discovered, was largely written by Jews to Jews about the Jews' Messiah, Jesus. Gentile believers should never forget that the founders of the church were Jewish. We owe the church to the Jew.

NOTES

1. Daniel Juster, *Jewish Roots* (Shippensburg, PA: Destiny Image Publishers, 1995), p. 135ff.
2. David H. Stern, *Messianic Jewish Manifesto* (Clarkesville, MD: Jewish New Testament Publications, 1991), p. 52.
3. Harold A. Sevener, *A Rabbi's Vision*, Chosen People Ministries, 1994, p. 1.
4. Kai Kjaer, *Joseph Rabinowitz and the Messianic Movement* (Grand Rapids: Wm. B. Eerdmans, 1995).
5. "My Pilgrimage: The Last Fifty Years," *Missionary Monthly*, January 1997, p. 8.
6. Juster, p. 148.
7. Charles R. Erdman, *An Exposition—the Acts* (Philadelphia: The Westminster Press, 1919), p. 145.
8. Stern, pp. 197-198.

6

A Day That
Is Different

The front page of the *New York Times* on August 8, 1995, carried a picture of Jonathan Edwards of Britain sailing toward a record in the triple jump at the world championships the previous day at Goteborg, Sweden. Not only did he break his own world record, but became the first person to hop, step and jump beyond 60 feet. The picture was captioned, "Leaping Into Untouched Territory."

The son of an Anglican vicar and a devoutly Christian mother, Edwards grew up in an English Devonshire manse with deep respect for Sunday, a day reserved for rest and reflection. No academic studies were permitted, no exercise, and perhaps most difficult for this sportsminded lad, no watching English soccer matches on TV. Soon his faith equaled that of his parents' so that, as he developed into a world-class triple jumper, he observed a strict Sunday: no practice and no contests.

This resulted in some hard choices. He sat out the 1988 British championships when the triple jump fell on a Sunday. He also sat out the 1991 world championships in Tokyo despite his agent's attempt to sway him with the argument that Sunday in Japan would be Saturday in England.

He was doubtless influenced by the example of Eric Liddell who inspired the Oscar-winning film, "Chariots of

Fire." In the 1924 summer Olympics, Liddell, a committed Christian, refused to run in the 100 meters because the qualifying heats fell on a Sunday. Favored to win the 100, and though untrained in the 400 meters, he nevertheless switched events and ended up winning the 400. But sadly in the specialization of the 90s, Edwards was competent only in the triple jump.

However, in 1993, he relented when a fellow Christian athlete, who had always run on Sunday retired. Edwards felt that it was now up to him to carry the Christian torch. He explained, "I decided it was my job to be at all the meets to be a Christian witness. I am doing what I feel God is telling me to do." His decision coincided with the best season of his career, as he won a bronze medal in the world championship and jumped to his personal best.

Then Edwards suffered a setback. Feeling sluggish and out of sort, and finishing poorly in some meets, he checked into a hospital and discovered he had the Epstein-Barr virus, one of the causes of mononucleosis. After several months of rest he resumed practice in 1995. Regaining his form, he set a British national record on June 11, a Sunday of all days. Then two Sundays later Edwards became the first man to go past 60 feet, only to have his jump declared ineligible because of a persistent wind, slightly above the permitted level. Then came his legitimately recognized world record in Goteborg.

Commenting on the days when he refused to run on Sunday, Edwards says, "It wasn't exactly my religion that kept me from competing. It was more that I wanted to keep Sunday different."

For millions of people in many parts of the world, Sunday is a day that is different. Some worship. Others scour the "Weekend" section of their newspapers in their urge for fun and diversion to the total neglect of the spiritual. Still others make it a combination of rest and recreation. But one way or another Sunday is observed differently from the other days of the week. And the reason for the observance of a day each week goes back to the God-given command to the Jews to "remember the Sabbath day to keep it holy." Though through the centuries Christians have generally kept Sunday, the first day of the week, and not Saturday, the Jewish Sabbath, the principle of Sunday observance can be traced to the practice of the Jewish Sabbath.

This same principle even extends beyond Christians and Jews to Muslims. Thea B. Van Halsema relates an exciting answer to prayer back in the mid 90s in getting her Middle East Witness Tour group into Egypt in the nick of time when their entrance was blocked by a change in visa policy which had just gone into effect a few days earlier. Crossing from southern Israel into Egypt at the Taba border checkpoint on a Friday morning, they learned that visas obtained at this checkpoint were valid for entering only the Sinai peninsula, not the whole of Egypt as formerly. Though en route to Mt. Sinai, they also wanted to go on to Cairo for a Sunday meeting with Christians and subsequent sightseeing. It was then ten o'clock. At eleven the consulate would close for the weekend.

Egyptian border officials said that if passports were brought to the Egyptian consulate in Eilat, the Israeli border city, they would be processed for entry into Egypt immediately. With some members of the group waiting, the leaders found a taxi to drive them the five miles to Eilat. After some anxious moments dealing with reluctant border officials, earnest praying, the hasty securing of passport photos, the filling out of lengthy forms, rushing to a quick copy place, and a speedy return taxi ride, the 25 visas were completed just before the officials closed the door at eleven A.M. The reason for the long weekend, explained Egyptian border officials soberly, was that Friday is holy day for Muslims, Saturday is Sabbath for Jews, and Sunday is worship day for Christians.[1]

THE SEVEN-DAY CYCLE HAS JEWISH ORIGINS

Old Testament scholar Arthur Lewis, in personal correspondence to my question as to whether other nations observed one day in seven replied, "The answer is No! Babylonians and others gave special honor to the day of the 'New Moon,' but this was the 15th day of the month and not a weekly day of rest as God ordered through Moses." Those who suggest that the observance of one day in seven is related to the lunar month should be reminded that the month is not composed precisely of four equal weeks, but has a day or so left over, so that the appearance of the new moon would be on a different day each month. The observance of one day in seven seems not to be traceable to the Babylonian calendar, but goes back to the Jewish nation.

Dan Juster said, "Only Israel had a seven-day cycle of weeks. We do not sense today how unique Israel truly was, for the seven-day week has since become the practice of the world."[2] Max I. Dimont pointed out that "The Greeks and Romans, who mercilessly worked man and beast seven days a week and called it industry, looked with scorn on the Jewish practice of a day of rest every seventh day for freeman, slave, and animal."[3]

THE SABBATH—A DIFFERENT DAY FOR JEWS

Today there are 39 basic categories of creative work banned on the Sabbath in Judaism, some of which are explicitly forbidden in the Old Testament: (1) baking and cooking (Ex. 16:23), (2) ploughing, harvesting, and reaping (Ex.

34:21), (3) kindling a fire (Ex. 35:3), (4) buying and selling (Neh. 13:15-17). These forbidden areas were expanded by Jewish scholars and applied to all sorts of circumstances arising over the centuries, which today form a considerable body of commentary.

In Jesus' day many things were not permissible on the Sabbath, including rescuing a drowning person. If a man were bitten by a flea, he was to permit the flea to keep on biting, for trying to counter the flea would make the man guilty of the sin of hunting on the Sabbath. Untying knots which needed only one hand for unraveling was permissible, but the use of two hands was work and forbidden.

Jesus found Himself repeatedly in conflict with the Pharisees over His failure to obey their strictures. He healed the sick and allowed His disciples to pick grain on the Sabbath—forbidden work.

One of my seminary professors, on a visit to Israel, asked a Hebrew scholar for his autograph. The scholar refused, because writing two consecutive words was not permissible on the Sabbath. Moments later in the heat of discussion the Hebrew scholar saw no inconsistency in climbing three rungs of a ladder in his library for a book to reinforce a point he was making.

In Judaism a joyous atmosphere was to prevail on the Sabbath. At one time, people were to have two complete changes of attire, one for weekdays, but one exclusively for the Sabbath. It was permissible to sleep a little longer that day. Knives sharpened in advance would add to the enjoyment of Sabbath food, most of which was to be prepared in advance of that day. The Sabbath was definitely a day that was different. Hyman E. Goldin described the Sabbath as "the most beautiful gift Israel received from God—the day of rest, which was in later years adopted by the rest of the world."[4]

The Sabbath is observed strictly in Israel today. Observant Jews are prohibited from picking up a phone or turning on a light. Either act violates the Halacha, the ancient rabbinic law which forbids even minor forms of work from sunset on Friday to sundown on Saturday. *Newsweek* reported that for years enterprising Jews have found ways around some of the bans. For example, many Israeli hotels and apartment-building elevators are rigged to stop automatically at every floor, thus sparing the devout the transgression of pushing buttons on the Sabbath. And electric ranges have a special Sabbath setting which keeps food hot without users having to turn on the heating element.[5]

SUNDAY—FOR CHRISTIANS A DAY THAT IS DIFFERENT

Christians have observed Sunday as a day of worship from earliest times. All four Gospel writers emphasize the first day of the week in connection with the resurrection of Jesus. No other event recorded in the four Gospels is so connected with a definite day of the week as is the resurrection. Ample documentary evidence indicates that the early church observed the first day. Ignatius, writing around A.D. 107, said, "They who walked in ancient customs came to a new hope, no longer living for the Sabbath, but for the Lord's Day, on which also our Light arose."[6] The term, "Lord's Day," was used by the apostle John to refer to the day on which, during meditation on spiritual matters on the Isle of Patmos, he was given a vision of the Lord Jesus Christ (Rev. 1:9). The expression, "Lord's Day" is not "the day of the Lord" but literally the "Lordly day."

Another early post-apostolic letter, dated not later than A.D. 130, stated, "We also celebrate with gladness the eighth day, whereon indeed Jesus rose from the dead."[7] When Emperor Constantine in the fourth century declared Sunday the day to be observed, he was only putting official approval on a day which had already been set aside for some 300 years.

Martin Luther would later declare, "We Christians . . . have the liberty to turn Monday or some other day of the week into Sunday if the Sabbath or Sunday does not please us."[8] Luther doubtless had in mind Paul's remarks, "One man considers one day more sacred than another; another man considers every day alike. Each one should be fully convinced in his own mind" (Rom 14:5). Also, Paul declared the Christian's liberty from Sabbath law in his epistle to the Colossian church, where some who combined incipient Gnosticism with Jewish legalism contended for a Christian observance of the Sabbath. Paul strongly repudiated this claim, "Do not let anyone judge you by what you eat or drink, or with regard to a religious festival, a New Moon celebration or a Sabbath day"(Col. 2:16).

Today some in the church believe that Sunday has replaced the Sabbath, and some do not. However, those who do not believe in Sunday as Sabbath replacement have found that Sunday is the expedient and appropriate day to keep voluntarily as a rallying time for corporate celebration of the resurrection. Both viewpoints see Sunday as special.

However, through the years Sunday observers have been just as much to blame at erecting a wall of restrictions on Sunday practices as the Pharisees were for their Sabbath. At one time families were not allowed to sweep or dust the house, make the beds, or cook on Sunday. In Scotland in the 17th century, one poor fellow was hailed into court for smiling on Sunday. Jonathan Edwards once resolved never to utter anything humorous on the Lord's Day. One family was obliged to eat pancakes that had been made on Saturday.

Sunday restrictions have produced a few oddities. Around 1875 the city of Evanston, Illinois, included among their Sunday prohibitions, called Blue Laws, a regulation forbidding the sale of ice cream sodas on that day. Some ingenious person thought of serving ice cream with syrup but no soda water. This Sunday delicacy became quite popular, so that on weekdays many asked for Sundays. City officials objected to naming the dish after the holy day, so changed the spelling. Sundae it has been ever since.

Those who want to remove the bath from sabbath, and the sun from Sunday find it difficult to be consistent. A missionary, visiting a supporting church on home leave, was rebuked by his hostess for typing correspondence on Sunday. Later the same afternoon the missionary found his hostess penning a letter. Some summer Bible conferences and camps who used to close the beaches and tennis courts on Sunday have changed their policy.

NOW IT'S THE WEEKEND

John D. Rockefeller, founding father of the millionaire family dynasty, loved ice-skating. Yet he would never skate on Sunday or let workmen flood his yard till a minute after midnight Monday morning. Three generations later, a commentator remarked, "It takes real application to get through the mammoth *New York Times,* attend church, play 18 holes of golf, catch the second game of a TV doubleheader, pick up the *60 Minutes* show, and then grab a late snack before getting a good night's sleep in preparation for a fruitful Monday." Today, a Sabbath day's journey is twice around the golf course.

Noting such radical change in Sunday observance led someone to remark, "Our great-grandfathers called it the Holy Sabbath; our grandfathers, the Sabbath; our fathers, Sunday; but today we call it the weekend. And many think it's getting weaker all the time."

A book called *The Weekenders* points out that the weekend in America has become its moment of hope. Every Friday night a national transformation takes place as people head home for a couple days of respite from their jobs. The weekend break may involve work around the house and yard, parties, dinners, movies, or trips. But do weekenders find what they seek? Loaded with fatigue, many of them are filled instead with lonely post-weekend blues—a sort of weekend hangover—feeling that they have lost something. The rich, full life they had dreamed about last Friday has eluded them, and they have to face Monday again. Whenever a holiday falls on Monday, giving an extra day, many discover that a three-day weekend merely turns Tuesday into Monday.

The book pointed out that such depression is not as likely to set in with people who plan their weekend activity in advance, and gave examples of ways that people spend weekends. A pretty secretary performs stunts on the wings of a speeding biplane before an admiring crowd. A life-insurance salesman wades for hours with his two boys in icy streams, panning for gold. A doctor splints and prunes trees for his neighbors. A lady-author conducts guided tours of the landmarks of her home town.

One author, who takes her family on weekend archaeological trips says, "Weekends are potential vacations. The average employee has about five times as much weekend time each year as he has for his entire vacation. Add it up! It's at least 104 days, not counting holidays."

Enthusiasts point out that weekends offer definite advantages over full-length vacations. The cost is not as great, planning is simpler, and it's easier to leave children with relatives for just a few days than for several weeks. But the big advantage is variety. You can do 52 different things on the weekends in one year.

Some people show considerable initiative in the ways they use their weekend time. But in the midst of all the above proposals one serious omission stands out like a sore thumb. Never do we hear the suggestion that people ought to go to their place of worship on weekends. For many, Sunday has become a national holiday instead of a holy day. Perhaps Sunday observance was too strict a century ago, but we have certainly swung the pendulum to the opposite extreme. Today literally millions of people spend weekends as though God did not exist.

A commentary in Dr. James Dobson's *Focus on the Family Bulletin* notes America's failure to observe and appreciate the "Day with a Difference": " If George Gallup polled people on their support for the Ten Commandments, most of the tenets would do rather well. We still endorse the ideals of honoring one's parents, not murdering, not lying, having no idols, and not committing adultery. The biggest exception would be this thing about the Sabbath. Very outdated, some people would say. A special holy day? Come on. Didn't that lead to all kinds of legalism, till it got so bad Jesus had to come along and do all kinds of 'forbidden' things on the Sabbath?

"Well, not entirely. He did poke holes in all the rule books and criticize those who refused to help a needy person because it was the Sabbath. But in His own personal life the day still meant something. Luke 4:16 tells us that going to worship was part of His weekly rhythm. He didn't stop to debate each weekend, 'Shall I, or shall I not?' Jesus set His pattern, and stuck to it, and so should we."[9]

IMPORTANCE OF A DAY
THAT IS DIFFERENT

The Sabbath was a central part of Jewish life. Its celebration testified to the lordship of God over creation. It contributed to Israel's physical and spiritual welfare through weekly rest, worship, evaluation, and renewal. The Sabbath was made for man, and not man for the Sabbath. For the Jew it was a sign of the covenant between God and Israel. It was a memorial of deliverance from slavery and a foretaste of the rest of faith. Without the Sabbath there would have been no synagogue. More than Israel keeping the Sabbath, the Sabbath kept Israel through the centuries.

The idea of the Sabbath was extended to the land. During the sabbatical year, observed every seventh year, the land remained fallow, and thus hopefully more fruitful the following years. The concept has influenced academic life, where the term "sabbatical" refers to a leave of absence with pay, granted to a college professor after several years of devoted teaching, for travel, research, or rest. Though originally granted the seventh year, now sabbatical leave refers to any time the leave is awarded. And its meaning is stretched to include any significant rest or change from routine in other walks of life.

A book titled *Taking Time Off* relates the stories of numerous students who, bogged down, disinterested, burnt out, or uncertain as to their purpose in life, enjoyed successful breaks from college to rediscover direction. The author likened taking a year or two off from academia to the sabbatical tradition which "grew out of the Judeo-Christian observance of the Sabbath on the seventh day of the week. The Sabbath is designed to rejuvenate and replenish—to bring people back to the rest of the week with a whole new perspective. Taking time off from school may do the same for you."[10]

The keeping of Sunday has great physical and spiritual values for Christians. Physically we need a change; a rundown person is an unproductive person. Sunday closing of businesses, though observed by a decreasing segment of the commercial community, is mainly on humanitarian grounds. Someone quipped, "The best insurance against car accidents is a Sunday afternoon nap."

But rest need not be equated with inactivity. The burdensome labor of earlier generations made the need for sheer physical rest on Sunday more acute than today. With many occupations not physically demanding, relaxation might be better secured by physical recreation. Each individual must answer for himself whether or not his Sunday activity makes him return to work Monday more rested or more tired than when he came home Friday.

Dr. Frank E. Gabelein, former headmaster of Stony Brook School and a *Christianity Today* editor, suggested cultural contemplation with discrimination, using Paul's criterion of "whatsoever things are true...and lovely" (Phil. 4:8) as fit exercise for a Christian's Sunday. A vesper program, piano recital, chamber music, art exhibit, visit to a museum, or drive through picturesque scenery would qualify in this category. Family get-togethers on Sunday bring delight, as sons and daughters return for a meal, permitting grandchildren to get acquainted with their grandparents. Sunday afternoon may provide an opportune time to start study for next Sunday's Sunday school lesson, or to read Christian literature.

The New Testament strongly urges helping others in a practical way. What better way to utilize a free hour on the Lord's Day than to visit the sick, needy, sorrowing, shut-in, nursing homes or prisons? Jesus set the example by often healing on the Sabbath in spite of severe criticism. These practices will help describe Sunday in the words of a hymn, "O day of rest and gladness, O day of joy and light."

But certainly Sunday is preeminently a day for worship. A questionnaire mailed out by a church asked, "How far do you live from the church?" and "How long does it take you to get to church?" One member answered, "I live about 4 blocks from the church, and to get there it takes me about 6 months." Some go once a year, on Easter, to commemorate the resurrection of Christ. A cartoon showed a pastor greeting people after the Easter service and asking once-a-year visitors. "Aren't you curious about what goes on here between Easters?" In reality, every Sunday morning should find us repeating to ourselves the words of the hymn writer, Isaac Watts:

"This is the day when Christ arose
So early from the dead;
Why should I keep my eyelids closed,
And waste my time in bed?"

On Sundays the early church took time to worship, study the Scriptures, fellowship, pray, sing, give, encourage one another, and observe the Lord's Supper. Those who call themselves Christians today ought to attend church regularly. We owe God homage and praise—Him from Whom all blessings flow—including the blessing of health and strength. We go to recognize Him in prayer, praise Him in song, acknowledge that He is worthy of adoration, confess our unworthiness, and thank Him for all His grace and goodness. Faithfulness in church participation witnesses to our contemporaries the reality of both what Jesus has done, and will yet do.

Another reason Christians ought to go to church regularly is because God commands it. Here is an unmistakable word of caution from the New Testament to every professing believer: "Let us not give up meeting together, as some are in the habit of doing" (Heb. 10:25). Churchgoing is not left to human whim; it is a divine must.

Since we are creatures of eternity as well as of time, and since we are to live by every word of God as well as by bread, we need the spiritual sustenance that comes from assembling with other saints. Sunday, above all other days, normally provides the leisure and opportunity to hear those truths to tell us how best to run our life.

A weekend at the ocean, or at a museum or historic battleground may be somewhat therapeutic, but it cannot bring healing to man's deepest needs. If we wish to get the most out of our weekends, church attendance with its inherent, imperishable values is indispensable. Sunday is the day that sees us "safely through another week." If we lose Sunday we lose our finest opportunity to worship God, serve our fellowmen, and bring refreshment to ourselves. One leader said, "Show me a nation that has given up the Sabbath and I will show you a nation that has the seeds of decay."

An elderly lady who worked hard washing floors six mornings a week was on her way to Sunday morning church. A friend who knew how hard she worked asked, "Wouldn't it be better for you to sleep late on Sunday morning? Wouldn't it help you keep going?" The lady leaned back on her heels and exclaimed, "It's going to church on Sunday that keeps me going the other six days of the week!" Your Sunday—if you make it a day that is properly different—will determine your week. More than that—your months, your years, your eternity.

Thomas Cahill calls the principle of a weekly rest the "innovation of the weekend, which got its start in the Jewish Sabbath (or 'Ceasing'). No ancient society before the Jews had a day of rest. The God who made the universe and rested bids us do the same, calling us to a weekly restoration of prayer, study, and recreation." Calling the Sabbath one of the simplest and sanest admonitions ever made, Cahill suggests that those whose schedules do not include "such septimanal punctuation are emptier and less resourceful."[11]

This principle of observing a day each week we owe to the Jews, who introduced it as a special covenant with God, and have kept it faithfully for 3,000 years.

NOTES

1. Thea B. Van Halsema, *Missionary Monthly*, August-September 1995.
2. Daniel Juster, *Jewish Roots*, pp. 15-16.
3. Max I. Dimont, *Jews, God and History*, p. 111.
4. Hyman E. Goldin, *The Jewish Woman and Her Home* (New York: Hebrew Publishing Co., 1941), pp. 115-116.
5. *Newsweek*, November 24, 1980, p. 114.
6. *To the Magnesians*, chapter 9.
7. *The Epistle of Barnabas*.
8. Martin Luther, Sermon, October 5, 1544.
9. James Dobson, *Focus on the Family Bulletin*, June 1995.
10. Colin Hall and Ron Lieber, *Taking Time Off* (New York: Noonday, 1996), p. 8.
11. Thomas Cahill, *Gifts*, p. 144.

7

The Messiah

During the early persecution of the Jews in Nazi Germany, some Jews began going to churches on Sunday. The Nazis sent orders to church leaders to ask the Jews to leave. Someone has related that in the middle of one service a pastor asked the folks to bow their heads and all who had Jewish fathers to leave. There was some rustling. Then the pastor asked all who had Jewish mothers to leave. Louder commotion. When the congregation looked up, someone had removed the form on the cross.

We owe the Messiah to the Jews. In His humanity He was Jewish. He was born in the Jewish city of Bethlehem, David's city, of a Jewish mother. He was a descendent of Abraham, Isaac, Jacob, and David. He was called "The Lion of the Tribe of Judah." He bore the Jewish name of Jesus.

He never left the confines of Palestine, except briefly as an infant carried in flight by his parents to Egypt. He spoke the Hebrew dialect of His day. He attended the Jewish synagogue and temple services and participated in the yearly festivals. For thirty years He lived in a Jewish home. When He began His ministry, He was recognized as a Jew. The Samaritan woman at Jacob's well asked in surprise, "You are a Jew and I am a Samaritan woman. How can you ask me for a drink?" (Jhn. 4:9). The superscription on the cross read, "Jesus of Nazareth, the king of the Jews (Jhn. 19:19). He was bone of their bone, and flesh of their flesh. Paul said that from the patriarchs "is traced the human ancestry of Christ, who is God over all, forever praised!" (Rom. 9:5).

Max I. Reich, a Jewish professor during my student days at Moody Bible Institute, penned these words,

> " They meant to shame me, calling me a Jew!
> I pity them. They know not what they do.
> They little think the name which they deride,
> Each time I hear it fills my heart with pride.
> Since Jesus bore that name when here on earth
> No princely title carries half such worth."

HANDEL'S MESSIAH

Recently my wife and I were looking around a gift shop filled with Christmas decorations. Suddenly above the din of friendly conversation I heard the strains of faint music over the store's sound system. I caught these words, "unto us a Child is born; unto us a Son is given, and the government shall be upon His shoulder, and His name shall be called Wonderful, Counselor, the Mighty God, the Everlasting Father, the Prince of Peace." I knew I was listening to *The Messiah.* I rejoiced in the almost universal acclaim given this oratorio sung every December in countless churches and played in shopping malls everywhere. I thought of how its composer, Handel, at the lowest ebb in his life, sequestered in his attic study for 24 days, often going without food and sleep, wrote almost continuously to capture the glorious music often called "The Greatest Story Ever Sung."

Every word of *The Messiah* is from the Bible. Listening to this oratorio, you hear only God's Word sung, for it's a compilation of verses drawn entirely from Holy Writ, predictions or fulfillments of the Anointed One. More verses come from the Old Testament than from the New. More than one-fifth of the Bible books are quoted, seven from the

Old, and seven from the New. Most quoted Old Testament books are Isaiah and Psalms. *The Messiah* is about the Messiah.

Two strains of seeming opposing thought run throughout this oratorio. First is the suffering, the humiliation, and the disavowal of the Messiah. "He was despised and rejected of men; a man of sorrows, and acquainted with grief. He gave His back to smiters, and His cheeks to them that plucked off the hair. He hid not His face from shame and spitting.... He was wounded for our transgressions; He was bruised for our iniquities." Reportedly, a visitor who arrived while Handel was writing this section found the composer shaking with emotion.

The second strain found in *The Messiah* is a glorious one, predicting the ultimate triumph and reign of the Lord Jesus Christ. The resurrection is promised in these lines, "But Thou didst not leave His soul in hell; nor didst Thou suffer Thy Holy one to see corruption." Also in "I know that my Redeemer liveth, and that He shall stand at the latter day upon the earth." But the most thrilling section of The Messiah for most folks is the "Hallelujah Chorus" as it exclaims over and over again, "And He shall reign for ever and ever, King of Kings, and Lord of Lords."

How sad that people, hearing *The Messiah* sung, fail to grasp the significance of these verses from the Bible. John Newton, once a slave trader and best known for his hymn "Amazing Grace," was converted seven years after the composition of this famous work. He grew to admire this oratorio, but with its rising popularity recoiled at the thought of people finding enjoyment in the music while totally heedless of the message. As a pastor, he delivered a series of "Fifty Expository Discourses on the Scriptural Oratorio,' praying that audiences would respond with a sense of obligation to the divine love that sent the Messiah.

THE MESSIAH—PREDICTION
AND FULFILLMENT

The inspiring compilation of texts in *The Messiah* doesn't begin to exhaust the Old Testament predictions about His coming. The Old Testament contains dozens and dozens of such prophecies. Dr. John Gerstner, professor at Pittsburgh Theological Seminary, quoted Church of England Canon Liddon as stating that "there are in all more than three hundred prophecies in the Old Testament concerning the coming Messiah. All have been fulfilled, more or less fully and clearly, in Jesus of Nazareth."[1]

Many times in the Gospels, events in the life of Jesus are mentioned as specifically fulfilling an Old Testament prophecy. For example, the account of His virgin birth (Matt. 1:22,23) is said "to fulfill what the Lord had said through the prophet." Then follows a quote from Isaiah 7:14, "The virgin will be with child and will give birth to a son, and they will call him Immanuel." The birthplace of Jesus— Bethlehem—was predicted over 500 years in advance. When the wise men came to Jerusalem seeking a newborn king, King Herod was disturbed at the mention of a rival, and asked the teachers of the law where the Christ was to be born. "In Bethlehem in Judea," they replied, "for this is what the prophet has written." To Herod they then quoted Micah 5:2: "But you, Bethlehem, in the land of Judah, are by no means least among the rulers of Judah; for out of you will come a ruler who will be the shepherd of my people Israel" (Matt. 2:1-6).

The flight of Joseph and Mary with baby Jesus to escape Herod's slaughter of innocent infants (Matt. 2:13-15) is said to fulfill what the Lord had said through the prophet Hosea (11:1), "Out of Egypt I called my son."

The senseless murder of baby boys (Matt. 2:16,17) fulfilled Jer. 31:15, which Matthew quoted. (From here on, we'll give just the reference of the prophecy and omit the quote.) In a Sabbath service in his hometown synagogue of Nazareth, Jesus read a prophecy about the Spirit's anointing of the Messiah for a ministry to the poor, to prisoners, and to the blind and the oppressed (Luke 4:16-21). Then with all eyes focused on Him, Jesus declared, "Today this Scripture is fulfilled in your hearing." He had quoted the prophet Isaiah (61:1,2).

The moving of Jesus from Nazareth to Capernaum, which was situated by the lake near Zebulun and Naphtali (Matt. 4:12-16) fulfilled a prophecy by Isaiah (9:1,2).

His plentiful use of parables (Matt. 13:34,35) was predicted in Ps. 78:2. Failure of the people to believe in Jesus even after performing many miracles in their presence (Jhn. 12:37), fulfilled Isaiah's prophecy (53:1).

Betrayal by one of His own (Jhn. 13:18-39) fulfilled a prophecy of David (Psalm 41:9).

Hatred against Jesus without any cause (Jhn. 15:24) was predicted by David in two Psalms (35:19; 69:4).

Jesus riding into Jerusalem on a colt in His so-called triumphal entry on the day we call Palm Sunday (Matt. 21:4,5) was foretold hundreds of years before by the prophet Zechariah (9:9).

The use of the thirty pieces of silver given Judas for betraying Jesus to purchase a potter's field (Matt. 27:3-10) was also foretold by the prophet Zechariah (11:12,13).

The division of Jesus' garments by the soldiers into four shares, and the casting of lots for His seamless robe (Jhn. 19:23,24) was foretold in another of David's Psalms (22:18)

The apostle John related that Jesus' cry, "I am thirsty" was uttered on purpose "so that the Scripture would be fulfilled" (19:28). The prophecy came from David's Psalm (69:21).

It was customary to break the legs of victims of crucifixion to hasten their death. Though the soldiers broke the legs of the thieves on either side of Jesus, they did not break His for they saw He was already dead. Instead, a soldier pierced His side with a spear, bringing a sudden flow of blood and water (Jhn. 19: 31-37). These actions, sparing His bones and piercing His side, fulfilled two prophecies (Psalm 22:17 and Zechariah 12:10).

Many predictions about Jesus are found in certain Psalms, termed by scholars "Messianic Psalms." Twice on the first Easter, first to the couple on the Emmaus road, and then to the disciples in the Upper Room, Jesus showed how the law of Moses, the Psalms, and the Prophets, predicted not only His death, but His glory as well (Luke 24:25-27, 44).

In Peter's sermon on the Day of Pentecost (Acts 2:24-35) he clearly declared that the resurrection of Jesus from the dead and His exaltation to the right hand of God had been prophesied by David (Psalm 16:8-11;110:1).

Two Messiahs had not been prophesied, one to suffer, and another to reign; rather, the one same Messiah was to both suffer and then be exalted. Paul's strategy in preaching in synagogues on his missionary journeys was to reason with his hearers from the Scriptures that the Messiah, when He came, had to suffer and rise from the dead. Then he would declare, "This Jesus I am proclaiming to you is the Christ" (Acts 17:1-3). His presentation rested strongly on Jesus' fulfillment of Old Testament prophecies.

Available in many Christian bookstores is the New Testament Prophecy Edition which notes in bold print verses that fulfill Old Testament prophecies about the Messiah. The Old Testament says, "The Messiah *will* come." The New Testament says, "The Messiah *has* come." Despite all the evidence to the Messiahship of Jesus, many believe that the Messiah has not yet come.

To those who hold that His coming is still future, Joseph Rabinowitz, pioneer of a Messianic congregation in

1885 in Russia, used to relate "The Parable of the Wheel," which went like this. Some people driving in a four-wheel wagon happened to lose a wheel. Finding that the wagon lurched along clumsily, they looked about and discovered that a wheel was missing. One of the men jumped down and ran *forward* in search of the missing wheel. To everyone he met he said, "We've lost a wheel. Have you seen a wheel?" Finally a wise bystander said, "You are looking in the wrong direction. Instead of looking in front for your wheel, you ought to be looking behind."

Then Rabinowitz commented that this was the same mistake Jews have been making for centuries. They have been looking ahead for the Messiah instead of looking back. The Messiah has already come. The four wheels of Hebrew history are Abraham, Moses, David, and Jesus. The Jews by looking in front, instead of behind, have failed to find their fourth wheel. Abraham, Moses and David are but beautiful types and symbols of Jesus. But thank God, "the Israelites of the New Covenant" have found Y'shua, our Brother Jesus, our All, "who of God has been made unto us, wisdom, righteousness, sanctification, and redemption;" from whom alone we have found divine light, life, liberty, and love, for the great Here and the greater Hereafter.[2]

THE BLOOD OF
THE LAMB

The Old Testament not only gave direct predictions of the coming Messiah, but also foreshadowed His death on the cross in many events involving sacrifices.

Right after Adam and Eve had sinned and stood in naked shame before a righteous God, the "Lord God made garments of skin for the pair and clothed them" (Gen. 3:21). They then learned that the covering for their sin came at a price—the death of an innocent substitute—the shedding of some animal's lifeblood.

Adam's sons, Cain and Abel, each brought an offering to the Lord. The Lord rejected Cain's, but accepted Abel's. Abel had offered portions of his flock. Through the shedding of blood, "by faith Abel offered God a better sacrifice than Cain did" (Heb. 11:4).

When the Lord was about to deliver the Israelites from Egyptian bondage, he directed the Jews to slay a lamb, and sprinkle its blood on their doorframes. The Lord said, "when I see the blood, I will pass over you" (Ex. 12:12,13). At midnight the Lord struck all the firstborn in Egypt. But every house that had the blood on the doorposts was passed over, and no one "under the blood" died. The lambs had died, but the sons were alive—saved by the blood of the lambs. This story foreshadowed the deliverance from sin's bondage for all who put their trust in the blood of the Messiah shed on Calvary. Paul wrote that "Christ, our Passover lamb, has been sacrificed" (I Cor. 5:7).

On Yom Kippur, the day of atonement, the High Priest required two goats. He would sacrifice one and sprinkle its blood on the Mercy Seat atop the Ark which contained the tablets of the Ten Commandments which the people had broken. On the head of the other goat the High Priest would lay both hands, confess the wickedness of the Israelites, and send it off into the desert. This annual ceremony anticipated the redemptive work of Jesus Christ who would first offer up Himself, shedding His blood as a sacrifice for our sins, and who also would carry away our sins never to be remembered against us again.

The book of Hebrews points out the finality of Jesus' sacrifice on the cross. Once He had offered Himself at Calvary and entered heaven to appear for us in God's presence, no further sacrifice was needed. "Nor did he enter heaven to offer himself again and again, the way the high priest enters the Most Holy Place every year with blood that is not his own....But now he has appeared once for all at the end of the ages to do away with sin by the sacrifice of himself" (9:25,26). The once-for-allness of Jesus' sacrifice was indicated by the ripping of the veil in front of the Holy Place. Just at the moment Jesus died, the curtain was torn from top to bottom (Matt. 27:51). The downward direction indicated a heavenly hand. Not only the Day of Atonement ceremony, but also the entire Levitical sacrificial system with its daily sacrifices, was done away with through the final, all-sufficient offering of the Lamb of God.

Priests must have sewed the curtain back together and used it till the temple was destroyed 40 years later. But other priests evidently saw a relationship between the tearing of the veil and the death of Jesus and became believers (Acts 6:7).

Of the various animals offered in Old Testament sacrifices, the lamb was probably the most frequent. So, it's not strange that "the Lamb" was a favorite title for the Lord Jesus. John the Baptist pointed Him out, "Look, the Lamb of God, who takes away the sin of the world!" (Jhn. 1:29). In the book of Revelation, He is called the Lamb over 25 times. John has a vision of "a lamb, looking as if it had been slain" (5:6). Revelation speaks of "the song of Moses the servant of God and the song of the Lamb" (15:3). Also of "the wedding supper of the Lamb" (19:9). Perhaps the most thrilling picture is that of the ten thousand times ten thousand circling the throne of God, where Jesus now sits, singing, "Worthy is the Lamb, who was slain, to receive power and wealth and wisdom and strength and honor and glory and praise."

Recently Messianic believers in Israel have pioneered the placing of full-page advertisements in the nation's leading Hebrew newspapers. The first, just before Yom Kippur in 1988, pictured a slain lamb on the Temple altar, and was headlined "Who Is The Sacrifice?" It explained to a poten-

tial audience of half the population of Israel how Y'shua
the Messiah atones for sin.

ISAIAH 53

Probably no Old Testament chapter speaks more clearly
beforehand of the humiliation, suffering and victory of the
Messiah than Isaiah 53. Here are snatches of the chapter:
"He was despised and rejected by men, a man of sorrows,
and familiar with suffering....we considered him stricken
by God, smitten by him, and afflicted. But he was pierced
for our transgressions, he was crushed for our iniquities;
the punishment that brought us peace was upon him, and
by his wounds we are healed. We all, like sheep, have gone
astray, each of us has turned to his own way; and the Lord
has laid on him the iniquity of us all. He was oppressed
and afflicted, yet he did not open his mouth; he was led
like a lamb to the slaughter, and as a sheep before her shear-
ers is silent, so he did not open his mouth....He was assigned
a grave with the wicked, and with the rich in his death,
though he had done no violence, nor was any deceit in his
mouth....my righteous servant will justify many....For he
bore the sin of many, and made intercession for the trans-
gressors."

Rabbinical scholars have tried to identify the Suffering
Servant of Isaiah 53 as the nation of Israel. But there are
some problems with this view. Isaiah 53 speaks of the Suffering Servant's perfect innocence, whereas Israel could
never be characterized as innocent. Also, the Servant suffers vicariously for the sins of others, whereas in the Old
Testament Israel suffers because of its own sin. Again, the
Servant suffers willingly, but the Old Testament never de-
scribes the sufferings of Israel as a willing sacrifice for the
sins of others, especially for the sins of Gentile people.

The language is so descriptive that it seems as though

THE MESSIAH

the prophet was standing by the cross reporting the proceedings. Interestingly, a few years ago some of our church teenagers told me of an incident in their high school where a section of the Bible was read over the loudspeaker each morning before classes. Because of a large Jewish enrollment, the agreement was that only the Old Testament would be read. One morning someone read Isaiah 53. A howl of protest went up from students claiming that the reading was from the New Testament and about Jesus!

The Ethiopian

It was Isaiah 53 that an important Ethiopian official was reading on his way home after worship in Jerusalem. Sitting in his chariot in the desert of Gaza, he was met by Philip, an evangelist, who had been diverted by an angel from evangelism in Samaria and directed to the Ethiopian's chariot.

Philip asked the Ethiopian if he understood what he was reading. "How can I," he said, "unless someone explains it to me," and then invited Philip to join him. The Ethiopian was reading the passage, "He was led like a sheep to the slaughter, and as a lamb before the shearer is silent, so he did not open his mouth." He asked who the prophet was talking about. "Philip began with that very passage of scripture and told him the good news about Jesus" (Acts 8:35). The Ethiopian believed and was baptized.

A Rabbi Believes

Through the centuries Isaiah 53 has led many to trust in Jesus as their Messiah. Harold A. Sevener details the conversion story of the founder of Chosen People Ministries.[3] Leopold Cohn, an orthodox rabbi from Hungary, in his search for the Messiah, left his wife and family to come to America. On his third Sunday in New York City, out for a walk, he saw a church sign in Hebrew saying, "Meeting for Jews." About to walk in, he was warned by friends not to

113

enter a building with a cross on top, "There are some apostates in that church who mislead our Jewish brethren. They say that the Messiah has already come." But since he was searching for the Messiah he went in.

Inside on the platform 24 Jewish girls, dressed in blue frocks with white sleeves, were singing in Yiddish with great sincerity and enthusiasm, "At the cross, at the cross, where I first saw the light." While he was pondering the enigma of Jewish girls singing about Jesus, the rabbi noticed that the room grew quiet, as if something exciting was about to happen. Suddenly, as if out of nowhere, a young man sprang onto the platform and without introduction began preaching about the Messiah. He ran back and forth across the platform with the force of a political orator. Suddenly he leaped to one side, disappeared into the wings, and in a few seconds came out again, carrying in his arms a little live lamb. The audience gasped. He went on with his sermon about the Lamb of God and the Lamb in Isaiah 53. Then the speaker, who was a Jew, went to the wings of the platform, handed the lamb over to another person, then came running out, shouting at the top of his voice, "The Messiah has come! The Messiah has come!" Though both fascinated and disgusted, the rabbi heard for the first time how salvation was available to all who believed in the Lamb of God, the Messiah.

Sometime later Leopold Cohn accepted Jesus as his Messiah and started a mission to Jews which, after a hundred years, is still going strong.

The book *Testimonies: of Jews who believe In Jesus*[4] contains the full accounts of how sixteen Jews came to believe in Jesus as their Messiah. Edited by Ruth Rosen, she chose to begin with the account of her mother's journey to faith. The following story is used with the publisher's permission.

Losing her mother in infancy, Ceil Rosen was raised in

an Orthodox Jewish home by foster parents who loved her and treated her as their own. They were strict about the dietary laws, kept all the holidays and forbad picking up a needle, scissors or even a pencil on Saturdays. She knew that being Jewish meant knowing the real God who expected things to be done in a certain way. She knew that unlike Jews, the goyim (non-Jews) had strange ideas about God. As observant as her foster parents were, she didn't hear much about God at home.

When she was 13, her mother moved to Denver because of her need for a better climate. At the age of questioning authority, Ceil tired under the restrictions of her Orthodox upbringing. When she was 14, she answered a knock at the door and found a boy named Moishe Rosen standing there, who was selling house numbers. Her mother didn't buy any, but Moishe asked her out on a date. She refused. A year later he asked again. At age 15 she went for a walk with him. They lived on the same block, went to the same school, and they began going steady. His family were nominally Orthodox, members of an Orthodox synagogue, but his mother didn't keep kosher. Ceil could eat bacon at his house and not feel guilty.

As a member of the high school girls' chorus, Ceil recalls them dressing up as Israeli women for a Christmas program, gliding across the floor in flowing gowns, and singing, "O come, O come Immanuel/ And ransom captive Israel." She suddenly realized that Jesus was Jewish, and briefly wondered if He could be for Jewish people after all.

Moishe and Ceil married when she was 18. They decided not to have an Orthodox home, but be modern American Jews without religious hang-ups. With pride in their heritage they maintained their roots, but the compulsion to be religious was lifted. Having her first baby at 19, she began saying prayers of thanks to God. Any doubts as to the existence of God evaporated. Though she didn't know what to believe about God, she knew He was the giver of life and in charge of things.

She and Moishe went to the movies a lot. The picture "Quo Vadis" made a lasting impression on her. Something about Jesus nabbed her attention. After Moishe gave her an album of Christmas carols which she listened to over and over, she asked herself, "Was it possible God really wanted her to believe in Jesus?" She began to wonder about the New Testament. She asked her cousin to buy a copy of the whole Bible at Newberry's 5 & 10. She read the four gospels, and then started all over again. She knew Jesus was real, and just couldn't read enough about Him. It was so obvious he was Jewish, and she was impressed with the down-to-earth, authoritative, compassionate way He talked.

Ceil knew that to confess Christ had the potential of disrupting family relationships. But she also knew that if Jesus' claims were true, then to deny Him would be to deny God. If she came to the conviction that Jesus was truly the Messiah, she would not be able to deny it, inconvenient and disruptive as it might be.

She wanted to talk to someone but didn't know where to turn. On a snowy day Mrs. Hannah Wago, a missionary, knocked on the door. A Christian lady, totally unaware of Ceil's search, had asked the missionary to visit the Rosens. Mrs. Wago began teaching every week but Moishe wanted no part of Ceil's growing interest. Finally, he told Ceil that Mrs. Wago was not welcome in their home. Ceil shifted their Bible studies to the telephone. One day Moishe came home to find Ceil engaged in one of their phone Bible studies. Moishe, who ordinarily would not deny Ceil anything, became so infuriated that he ripped the phone out of the wall. Embarrassed at his flash of anger, Moishe later apologized, but made no attempt to call a repairman. Ceil discreetly continued her studies with Mrs. Wago.

On Easter Sunday 1953, Ceil walked into a church for

the first time in her life. She responded to the invitation and came forward to pray with the minister. After that she prayed for her husband every day, weeping as she asked the Lord to show him the truth about Jesus. Seeing Ceil's deep interest, Moishe began reading about Jesus and could make quite a case against Christianity. But the information he had read had taken root. They both were surprised one Saturday night when Moishe confessed his faith. They both prayed for him to accept Jesus as his Messiah. He told Ceil he wanted to go to church the next day. He went forward at the minister's invitation, just as Ceil had on Easter.

They told both sets of parents who could not understand nor accept their children for believing in Jesus. Ceil's folks told her to forget that she was their daughter. They left town, and Ceil never saw them or heard from them again. She did hear that they moved to Israel, but could never discover any trace of them. Moishe's parents threatened to disown them, but did not cut them out of their lives for more than a year or so.

Says Ceil, "When I began praying that Moishe would accept Jesus as his Messiah, I had no idea what I was asking. Once my husband committed his life to Y'shua, he could not bear to stand idly by while the majority of our people went on believing that Jesus is only for Gentiles. My husband eventually became the founder and executive director of Jews for Jesus, a team of people who have challenged literally millions to think about Jesus."

Moishe Rosen says, "Witnessing to Jews is like Philip who, becoming a follower of Jesus, went and found Nathaniel. Like Philip, we want to find our brothers and sisters and tell them, 'We have found the one Moses wrote about in the Law, and about whom the prophets also wrote—Jesus of Nazareth, the son of Joseph.'"

Rosen has a suggested prayer to help Jews or Gentiles who wish to become followers of Jesus. "God of Abraham,

I know that I have sinned against You, and I want to turn from my sins. I believe you provided Jesus (Y'shua when speaking to Jews) as a once-and-for-all atonement for me. With this prayer I receive Jesus as my Savior and my Lord. I thank You for cleansing me of sin and making me a new person. Amen."

A well-to-do businessman was entertaining a devout believer in his palatial home. In the course of the evening, while the two of them were sitting in the living room before the glowing fireplace, the wealthy host, a nominal Christian, made a biased remark, "I want nothing Jewish in my home." The surprised guest said nothing at first. Then slowly rising from his chair, he approached a painting on the wall. It was the apostle Paul preaching to the Athenians on Mars Hill. Carefully he took the painting down and laid it by the crackling fireplace. Then spotting a lovely leather Bible on a marble table, he walked over, picked it up, and placed it beside the painting. Looking around, he saw a painting of the crucifixion, painstakingly removed it and laid it beside the Bible and the other painting. Then picking up all three items, and moving in the direction of the fireplace, he paused, "You said you want nothing Jewish in your home. Would you like me to put these in the fire?"

In a flash the host jumped to his feet. "Stop! Stop! May God forgive me! I never thought of it in this light before. I never realized how indebted I am for things Jewish—especially my Savior."

NOTES

1. John Gerstner, *Reasons for Faith* (New York: Harper
   & Row, 1960), p. 115.
2. Kai Kjaer, *Rabinowitz*, pp. 57-58.
3. Harold A. Sevener, *Vision*, pp. 7-11.
4. *Testimonies: of Jews who believe In Jesus*, ed. Ruth Rosen
   (San Francisco: Purple Pomegranate Productions, 1992),
   pp. 1-11.

8

Some Ways To Repay

In 1978 Dr. G. Douglas Young, founder and president of the Institute of Holy Land Studies in Jerusalem, was honored by the city with its highest award, "Worthy of Jerusalem." Those chosen for this title are traditionally over 70 and Jewish. Young was neither. The Mayor of Jerusalem made the presentation at a special convocation with the President of Israel present.

The citation mentioned his doctorate from Dropsie College, his books, his knowledge of the Hebrew language, his enthusiastic lecturing "of the Bible and of the study of the evangelical religion," his support of Israel and its right to exist, including a stint as ambulance driver in the six-day war.

Dr. Young taught Old Testament at U.S. seminaries until 1958, when he founded the Institute of Holy Land Studies in Jerusalem. Located first on the Street of the Prophets, and later on holy Mt. Zion, this was the first school in Jerusalem devoted to biblical studies on the American seminary level. Young utilized the first-rate scholarship of Israeli professors from the Hebrew University, and attracted hundreds of students from over fifty cooperating American institutions of higher learning.

He was the moving spirit behind the Jerusalem Conference on Biblical Prophecy in 1971, and the Congress for the Peace of Jerusalem in 1978. Retiring from the Institute in

121

1978, Young spent his remaining years heading up a new work in Jerusalem, Bridges for Peace, promoting Jewish-Christian relations. Why did Dr. Douglas Young spend so much of his energy to promote interest in the Jews? The answer is found in his own words, "We owe so much historically to the Jewish people."[1] He always challenged Christians to have the proper attitude toward Jews, and to work in concrete ways toward real friendship and mutual understanding. A book written on the life of Young is aptly titled, *A Gentile With the Heart of a Jew.*[2] Though none of us will ever likely possess the same degree of dedication, yet we should recognize, acknowledge, and begin to discharge our enormous obligation to the Jews. We suggest some ways.

SEEK FOR A GREATER UNDERSTANDING OF JEWISH PEOPLE

Young pointed out that just as Jews need to understand real Christianity, so, too, do Gentiles need to understand Jews.

Three major groups

Rabbi Yechiel Eckstein's *What Christians Should Know About Jews and Judaism*[3] tells us that Jews, worldwide, number about fourteen million; in the USA, about six million, who belong mainly to three groups: Reformed, Orthodox, and Conservative.

Reform or Liberal Judaism began in early nineteenth century Germany, and was the first to adapt the character of Judaism to a changing modern world. Its most serious break with the past was the rejection of the divine authority of the Torah (Pentateuch), and of the rabbinical tradition, holding these writings as not inspired of God but created by human genius. Drastic changes were introduced in synagogue worship, like men and women sitting together instead of separately, organ playing, the replacement of Hebrew with the vernacular, the elimination of several prayers, and in some temples the switching of the Sabbath from Saturday to Sunday. Many traditional precepts were also discarded, like belief in a physical, personal Messiah, the resurrection of the dead, and kosher dietary laws. They stressed the ethical teachings of the prophets. However, the eruption of the Holocaust and the birth of the state of Israel prompted a more traditional approach toward the issues of Torah, ritual, and Messianism. An estimated 30% of Jews in the USA are Reform.

Orthodox Judaism found a home for those who felt that the Reformers had gone too far from tradition. The Orthodox refused to compromise the strict observance of the law. Despite some differences dividing Orthodox Judaism, they are united in their belief in the divinity of the Bible, and in the binding authority of the Talmud and other forms of rabbinical literature. They are conservatives theologically, and often socially and politically. They embrace Zionism, and believe that God will send the Messiah to Israel. They claim about 12% of U.S. Jews.

Considered as part of the overall Orthodox movement are the 250,000 U.S. Hasidics who, rigidly loyal to the system of Jewish law, are known for their distinctive garb, sidelocks and beards. Some are considered anti-Zionist because they oppose the existence of the state of Israel until Messiah comes. One author claims they are growing at the rate of 5% per annum.[4]

Conservative Judaism has been described as a critique of both Reform and Orthodox. Many felt that the Reform advocated the abrogation of Jewish law, while the Orthodox was regarded as preoccupied with the law. To fill the void Conservative Judaism was born. This centrist school aimed at preserving traditional Judaism, yet adapting it to modern conditions through temperate change. It is not so much a creedal order as it is a peoplehood. Their middle-of-the-road position provides a rallying point for about 40% of American Jews.

It is estimated that about 10% of all Jews attend synagogue on a given Sabbath, and 70% only four times a year. About 30% in the USA are married to Gentiles.

Degrees of inspiration

When Jews talk about the Bible, they may mean something different from the evangelical concept. Whereas Orthodox Jews accept the entire Old Testament as inspired, other groups limit the Bible to only the first five books of Moses, the Pentateuch. In its broader sense the Torah means the Old Testament. In its limited sense the Torah means the Pentateuch. Orthodox Jews also believe that the Talmud, the Oral Law, was given by God to Moses on Mt. Sinai along with the Written Law, and is likewise binding.

Survival

The history of the Jews tells us much about a minority group's survival, despite several centuries of persecution, and without a homeland of their own. In the introduction to his book *Jews, God and History*, Max I. Dimont says that by all logic they should have disappeared a hundred times over, yet now have a state of their own. Frederick the Great reputedly asked his chaplain to give him one compelling evidence for the existence of God. The chaplain replied, "The amazing Jew, your Majesty."

The Romans destroyed Jerusalem in A.D. 70. The conquering Romans have vanished, but the Jews still live on.

Approximately six million Jews were killed in concentration camps during World War II. In spite of the carnage

Jewish history marches on. The Third Reich, which Hitler bragged would endure for a thousand years, disintegrated after twelve years. The Jews, whom Hitler boasted he would annihilate, survived to create a new, independent Jewish state. A study of Jewish history bears out God's promise to Abraham, "I will bless those who bless you, and whoever curses you I will curse" (Gen. 12:3).

A greater appreciation of our Jewish friends comes through learning more about their history, customs, beliefs, Sabbath, and practices related to the Jewish life cycle. Attendance at a Passover Seder with explanation of the various symbols can be most enlightening, as can a study of their annual festivals.

OPPOSE ANTI-SEMITISM

All around us lurks the insidious plague of anti-Semitism, often in little but shameful injustices. We can help repay our debt by opposing this dishonorable bias.

We should acknowledge the anti-Jewishness of
Christians through the centuries

Almost from its earliest years the church has been guilty of an anti-Jewish attitude. Though for the first few decades good relations existed between Jewish Christians and unbelieving Jews, at the destruction of Jerusalem in A.D. 70, the two groups went in different directions. Christians saw in the demolition of the Temple punishment on the Jews for killing their Messiah, and some later taught that the church had taken the place of the Jews.

Athanasius, Patriarch of Alexandria (died 373), a staunch defender of the deity of Christ, declared that "the Jews were no longer the people of God, but rulers of Sodom and Gomorrah," and that therefore they should not be allowed to continue in disbelief without punishment. This opened the door for attacks on unbelieving Jews.

St. Ambrose, Bishop of Milan (died 397), told his congregation that the local synagogue was a house of impiety, a receptacle of folly which God himself had condemned, and could be burned. His congregation burned the synagogue.

Chrysostom, the golden-mouthed orator of the fourth century, was loving toward mankind in general, but he wrote eight poisonous sermons against the Jews. It was he who coined the word "deicide" to apply to the Jewish people. He called the Jews a cursed nation that could never rise again, because for killing God there is no pardon.

Augustine, Bishop of Hippo and most influential theologian of the fourth century, made this most derogatory accusation, "The true image of the Hebrew is Judas Iscariot, who sells the Lord for silver. The Jew can never understand the scriptures and forever will bear the guilt for the death of Jesus."

Twelfth-century Bernard of Clairveaux, saintly as he was, claimed that the dispersion of the Jews to all regions was penalty for their great crime of crucifying Jesus.

When the Reformation divided Christendom, the Jews suffered havoc from both sides. A papal bull in 1555 condemned them to slavery because of their guilt in killing Christ; they had to live like animals in a compound (the ghetto); they had to sell all their properties outside the ghetto walls to Christians; they had to wear special clothing, were restricted to certain professions and trades. Often the choices were incarceration, death, exile, or coerced conversion. The latter was sometimes called the passport to European civilization. Fleeing from country to country earned them the descriptive "wandering Jew."

Though Martin Luther spoke kindly of the Jews in his earlier years, he turned against them when they continued to reject Christ. He wrote, "All the blood kindred of Christ burn in hell, and they are rightly served even according to their own words they spoke to Pilate. They should be forced to hardest labor as handymen of serfs only; they should not be permitted to hold services; every Christian should be admonished to deal with them in a merciless manner." It is said that Hitler quoted from this tirade in support of his program of extermination of Jews. With such a history of anti-Jewish attitudes and atrocities in the name of Christ and the church, is it any wonder that Jews do not find it easy to cozy up to those who call themselves Christians?

Perhaps, then, a first step in opposing anti-Semitism is acknowledgment of our past failures. In May, 1976, Dean Arthur F. Glasser and the School of World Mission faculty of Fuller Theological Seminary, on the occasion of Israel's celebration of its 28th anniversary, released a statement to the church at large, which reads in part, "We are profoundly grateful for the heritage given to us by the Jewish people which is so vital for our own Christian faith....We regret exceedingly that Christians have not always shared this Gospel with the Jewish people in a loving and ethical manner. Too often, while interested in Jewish evangelism in general, we have demeaned the dignity of the Jewish person by our unkind stereotyping and our disregard for Jewish sensitivities. How un-Christlike we have been!" [5]

We should avoid the use of certain words
and judgments

A rabbi from Chicago heard a minister friend, reporting on his trip to the Holy Land, tell how he had haggled with a merchant over the price of an item in a Jerusalem marketplace. Another minister asked, "Did you jew him down?"' Remarked the rabbi, "Knowing the minister as I do, I am certain that his comment did not reflect a deep-seated, unconscious contempt for Jews, because it was not the least bit characteristic of him to associate Jews in particular with cheating or haggling. Rather, I believe it came from a complete unawareness of the derivations and implications of his remark."

Many distinguish between anti-Jewishness and anti-Semitism. Most every nation has critics who dislike it. Statesmen are fully aware of anti-British, anti-American, anti-German, or anti-Jewish sentiment, sometimes deserved. But anti-Semitism, a pathological hatred of Jews which exceeds anti-Jewishness, is illogical, irrational, a psychological puzzle. It seeks out the Jewish race deliberately, excluding others who might be equally guilty, and has no solution, forgiveness, nor alternative. It is a paranoia that creeps so easily into our culture against imagined conspirators who control the business world, capitalism, the movie industry, Wall Street, television, the banking industry, or government. Michael Jackson's singing, "Jew me, sue me, everybody do me—kick me, kike me, don't you black or white me!" justly drew immediate objection.

Anti-Semitism leads to negative stereotyping, as in Europe in the Middle Ages when Jews were blamed for a contaminated water supply, or an epidemic of typhoid or the black plague. Jews became the scapegoat for the ills of society. No wonder the Anti-Defamation League came into existence. Today, you might hear, "The Holocaust never happened. That's Jewish propaganda!" A visit to the new Holocaust Museum in Washington, D.C. will readily refute such revision of history and confirm the reality of this gruesome tragedy.

We should make protest openly when necessary

In his book *Jews, Gentiles, and the Church*, David Larsen tells of a situation involving his own family. When school bus service was terminated in his community, and a projected car pool excluded a neighborhood Jewish boy, his wife protested. She was told by other parents that she and the

Jewish family could make their own plans.[6]

Larsen urges us to "steadfastly oppose this vicious plague of anti-Semitism wherever and whenever it rears its ugly face."[7]   He cites the sale of an anti-Semitic computer game in Europe in which players assume the role of a Nazi commandant of a concentration camp and then amass points for torture of prisoners, extracting gold from their teeth, making their skin into lampshades, and selling their remains for soap. This should certainly bring protest from concerned citizens.

Among the noblest of protesters of all times were those who protected Jews from the Nazi Holocaust. Imagine having a guest in your home for two months, even two years. Guests that were not even your friends, but strangers, perhaps even someone you disliked. Keeping them meant continuous, varied strategies of subterfuge on your part, and months of danger and stress, and if your deception were discovered or betrayed, you faced torture, prison, concentration camp, and death. The movie *Schindler's List* recounts the true story of an Austrian businessman who saved 1500 Jews from extermination in Nazi death camps.

Engraved on the wall of the Washington Holocaust Museum are the names of hundreds of brave men and women who saved tens of thousands of Jews from the Holocaust. Among them I saw the name of Corrie ten Boom, whose book and movie *The Hiding Place* tells how her family hid several Jews in a secret attic room till betrayed by a fellow-citizen. I'll never forget the thrill, as a pastor, of bringing her to speak to our church. As she stood there, at a frail 86, I thought of the fearless courage of the ten Boom family which lost a brother, father and sister in the Holocaust, simply because they protected Jews from the Nazis.

Another book *Rescuers: Portraits of Moral Courage in the Holocaust,*[8] tells the unforgettable stories of those who in the face of Nazi brutality hid Jews in cellars and behind false walls, shared their meager food rations, disposed of waste, smuggled people out of ghettos, and raised Jewish children as their own. This book was sponsored by the Foundation for Christian Rescuers, an organization dedicated to the honoring of Christians who rescued Jews during the Holocaust. Yad Vasehem, Israel's Holocaust research center has identified 11,000 rescuers by name and honored them with the title "Righteous Gentiles."

We should be ready to explain New Testament texts which are frequently interpreted as anti-Semitic

Several verses in the Gospel of John refers to "the Jews" who persecuted Jesus (5:16); tried to kill Him (5:18); were waiting to take his life (7:1); picked up stones to stone Him (10:31). Logical interpretation tells us that "Jews" in these and similar verses cannot mean all Jews. Not all Jews in Jerusalem wished Him killed. His disciples were Jews, including the author of the Gospel of John. Many Jews believed on Him, including the three thousand at Pentecost. At the time, over a million Jews, more than the population of Palestine, were scattered in the Diaspora, far from Jerusalem, unaware of and without any responsibility for the crucifixion. The term "the Jews" refers to their leaders. In fact, some modern versions render it "the leaders of the Jews." The Living Bible paraphrases it "Jewish leaders." Even among the leaders, not all sought to kill Him. Nicodemus and Joseph of Arimathea were in His corner. So all Jews should not be summarily charged with seeking to kill Him.

Through the centuries the charge of "Christkiller" has been flung at Jews, because at His trial the people called out, "Let his blood be on us, and on our children."(Matt. 27:25). The shouts of an angry mob cannot be binding on all. Besides, these words were put in their minds and mouths by their leaders. It is absurd to blame the Jews of all generations for the statement of a fraction of them in a mob frenzy. Many in that mob doubtless were among the 3,000 who repentantly accepted Jesus fifty days later. Had not Jesus prayed, "Father, forgive them, for they do not know what they are doing"? (Lk. 23:34). We don't hold all Americans today guilty for the death of Abraham Lincoln. True—some Jews were involved, so were some Romans (Acts 4:27). Really, we all share some of the guilt for His death—our sins helped crucify Him.

REFLECT ON THE FUTURE OF JEWISH PEOPLE

Though some theologians teach that the church has replaced Israel in God's prophetic scheme, many evangelical scholars hold to a literal fulfillment of blessing in the future of the Jews. And this hope is twofold. The first is physical—the Old Testament promises of the land. The second is spiritual—the New Testament promise of Israel's conversion—"All Israel will be saved" (Rom. 11:26).

The promise of the land

When Abraham answered the call of God, the Lord said to him in Canaan, "To your offspring I will give this land" (Gen. 12:7). Later he repeated the promise to Abraham, "Lift up your eyes from where you are and look north and south, east and west. All the land that you see I will give to you and your offspring forever" (13:14,15). See also 15:7, 17:8 and 24:7.

The Lord also made the same promise to Abraham's son, Isaac (Gen. 26:3,4). And to Jacob on his flight from Esau (28:13).

In dialogues between the Lord and Moses, reference is frequently made to the "promised land" (Ex. 12:25, 13:5,11; 32:13, 33:1). Joshua referred to it similarly (Josh. 23:5). The prophets warned Israel of expulsion because of disobedience, but also foretold of a return to the land from captivity. Isaiah spoke of a return "from all the nations" (43:5,6; 66:20). So did Jeremiah (12:15, 16:14,15, 23:5-8, 33:10-13).

Ezekiel foretold this double blessing. First, the land. "For I will take you out of the nations; I will gather you from all the countries and bring you back into your own land...." Second, the new spiritual life. "I will cleanse you from all your impurities....I will give you a new heart....I will put my Spirit in you and move you to follow my decrees and be careful to keep my laws" (Ezek. 36:24-27). The next chapter with its vision of the valley of dry bones coming to life, also indicates Israel's future as including both a return to the land and a spiritual renewal (37:11-14).

Other prophets played the same theme (Micah 2:12; Zeph. 3:19,20). Amos ends his prophecy, "I will bring back my exiled people Israel; they will rebuild the ruined cities and live in them....I will plant Israel in their own land, never again to be uprooted from the land I have given them" (9:14,15). The Psalmist spoke of this same promise (105: 8-11).

Some say these prophecies had to do with returning to their homeland after the earlier captivities. But the language often has a magnitude beyond anything that Israel historically experienced in the return from the Babylonian and Persian exiles. Interestingly, Benjamin Netanyahu, Prime Minister of Israel, in a recent interview with *Newsweek* on the eve of Israel's 50th anniversary, commented, "And in the next decade, a majority of Jewish people will live in the Jewish land. I'm not a religious person, but this is in some way a realization of the prophetic dream of the ingathering of Israel." [9]

As a boy in the 1930s I heard my pastor often say that the Jews would some day go back to their land. It seemed such an impossibility then. Yet a few years later, in 1948,

Israel was given its statehood, and despite the attacks on this fledgling state, it has emerged the most powerful force in the Middle East. In less than fifty years it has become a center for technical and scholarly research. The desert has indeed blossomed as the rose.

Is the return to the land a sign of the end times? Perhaps, but not necessarily. God does not move at our speed. He took centuries before, in the fullness of time, to send His Son down to the manger. But the stage is certainly set for His coming. If the Jews are back in the land, spiritual renewal may be not too far behind.

As part payment of their debt to the Jews, many Christians pray for the peace of Jerusalem. In early 1978 the International Congress for the Peace of Jerusalem was held in the city's Diplomat Hotel. Two months previous a full page ad was placed in the *New York Times* over the signature of fifteen leading evangelicals titled "Evangelical Concern For Israel." Main thrust of the ad was affirmation of the right of Israel to exist as a free and independent nation. Expressing concern about the welfare of all the countries of the Middle East, it declared "belief in the promise of the land to the Jewish people—a promise first made to Abraham and repeated throughout Scripture, a promise which has never been abrogated." They pledged to work for justice for all nations. Evangelicals shy away from blanket endorsement of every Israeli policy. Evangelicals believe in a balanced concern for Palestinian and other rights.

Interestingly, we are never directed to pray for Moscow, Beijing, London, Paris, Bonn, or Washington. But we are commanded to pray specifically for Jerusalem, a city which recently observed its 3,000th birthday. Says the Psalmist, "Pray for the peace of Jerusalem!" (122:6 RSV).

The conversion of Israel

Writing to the Romans, Paul states that, "Israel has experienced a hardening in part until the full number of the exiled Gentiles has come in. And so all Israel will be saved" (11:25,26). The apostle had argued that the stumbling of the Jews over the gospel was neither futile nor final. Because of Jewish rejection of the gospel, salvation came to the Gentiles, but then some day the nation of Israel, as a whole, would turn to Christ. He argued that if the rejection of Jesus by Jews had resulted in the salvation of Gentiles, what great spiritual benefit would result for Gentiles when Jews en masse turned and accepted Christ!

To illustrate his point Paul used the figure of an olive tree to represent Israel. Its roots contain Abraham, Isaac, and Jacob, named Israel, and the children of Israel or Jewish people. Nearby stood a wild olive tree, representing Gentiles, wild because they were alienated from the commonwealth of Israel, strangers to the covenant of promise, and without hope. When Jesus began to build His church, the olive tree was almost exclusively Jewish with tens of thousands of believing Jews in Jerusalem alone (Acts 21:20). But by the time Paul wrote this letter to the Romans it was evident that, for the most part, Jews were rejecting the good news, Paul likening them to branches of the cultivated tree now cut off. He likened Gentile believers to branches from the wild olive tree now grafted into the original olive tree. He warned them (Gentiles) not to boast for they could in turn be cut off like the original branches (Jews). And conversely, the cut-off branches (non-believing Jews) could be grafted in again if they came to faith. Then Paul emphasized that natural branches (Jews) will indeed be grafted back when "the full number of the Gentiles has come in." This extensive re-grafting is the conversion of "all Israel."

Exactly when this conversion takes place depends on one's prophetic viewpoint. Those who believe the church will be raptured before the Tribulation place the conversion of the Jews during the Tribulation. In the Post-tribulation view, the church would still be on earth when the conversion of Israel takes place, and would enjoy a great influx of new Jewish believers. The original olive tree would experience a massive re-grafting of original branches, and Jew and Gentile together would constitute the people of God. Whatever one's prophetic timetable or viewpoint, one certain factor is the conversion of Israel.

Dr. D. Martin Lloyd-Jones, famous English preacher, although not known for his prophetic themes, declared, "A day is coming when the bulk of the nation of Israel is going to believe the gospel.[10] Even some non-dispensational scholars, who hold that the church has replaced Israel, believe in a future removal of the scale from blinded Jewish eyes to reveal the One they had pierced, resulting in a large-scale reclamation of the Jews with a great impact on the Gentile world.

David Stern says the "all" in reference to a collective like "Israel" does not mean every single individual, but rather the main part, the essential part, or the considerable majority. "Therefore I believe that when 'all Israel' is saved, it will not be that every Jew believes in Yeshua, but that the Jewish nation will have a believing majority and/or a believing establishment."[11]

Today many wonder if the recent emergence of thousands and thousands of Messianic Jews may be a significant precursor in God's plan of saving all Israel.

SHARE THE GOSPEL WITH JEWS

The apostle Paul had a great passion for the salvation of his fellow-Jews, possessors of so many spiritual privileges (Rom. 9:1-5). Since the church has been the recipients of so many benefits through the Jews, Gentile believers should work for their evangelization. In their recent book *Witnessing to Jews,* Moishe and Ceil Rosen offer valuable insights culled from years on the cutting edge of relating the love of Jesus to fellow Jews. Significantly they say, "Statistics show that most Jewish believers first heard the gospel from a Gentile believer."[12]

Build bridges

If we would win any person, Jew or Gentile, we need to build bridges in their direction. To win friends to the Lord, we must have friends to win. One reason Dr. Douglas Young moved to Jerusalem and became an active member of the community was to build bridges. He wanted his students to do good work so that their Israeli professors would say, "Those Christians are great people." Young did establish a legitimate Christian presence and earned a respected hearing for the gospel, even from those who disagreed with his gospel message. A well-known Rabbi expressed appreciation for Young's ability to make his Christian convictions known without disparaging his (the Rabbi's). He volunteered that Young's quiet confidence in the New Testament had encouraged him to study it afresh.

Since Jews often invited him to their Passover Seder, he in turn at Christmas would invite neighbors for a turkey dinner. Going beyond a brief grace at the start of a fancy meal, Young invented a liturgy which included all the narratives in Matthew, Luke and all of John 1, including, "He came unto his own, and His own received Him not. But as many as received him, to them gave he the power to become the sons of God." He gave them the whole bit, including Christmas carols. Some of the nicest letters he received from Israeli Jews resulted from this kind of experience.

When Prime Minister Yitzhak Rabin was assassinated in 1995, many U.S. Christians sent notes of sympathy to the Embassy of Israel in Washington. This is bridge-building.

Friendships need to be cultivated with Jewish friends and neighbors.

Franz Mohr, the chief concert technician for piano maker Steinway and Sons for more than a quarter century, has been a close colleague of a host of such legendary musicians as Horowitz and Rubinstein. His book *My Life with the Great Pianists*[13] tells how he attended their instruments, made delicate adjustments, and had the opportunity to rub shoulders with them in an intimate way. He gave every pianist a Bible, and prayed for them faithfully. For years he prayed for an opening to share his faith with Horowitz, who was Jewish. One Sunday prior to a concert in Boston, Horowitz was practicing at the Sheraton when one of the notes would not perform properly for him. Someone suggested getting Mohr, who went along for every concert and was just across the street in a motor inn. Horowitz said, "Oh, don't bother him. I'm sure he's running after the girls of Boston."

Mohr's superior, who was present, became very serious, "Oh, Mr. Horowitz, you don't know Franz. He would never do that. Franz is a wonderful Christian fellow who loves his family, and I bet he's reading his Bible right now. He reads all the time." Horowitz was stunned at this answer, and said, "Call up Franz and ask him what he's doing." When the call came, "Franz, what are you doing?" Franz replied, "Well, I am reading my Bible and making notes for teaching my adult Bible class next week."

Franz came right over with his tools. Before he could put his bag down, Horowitz said, "Franz, tell me what is that you believe? They tell me that you read the Bible all the time. Tell me about that." Franz told the story of how he became a Christian as a boy in Nazi Germany, and how he was now a most contented person. Horowitz really listened. "Franz, that is some story. I am supposed to be Jewish, but I have nothing whatsoever of faith. My friends have never heard a story like this. If I invite you to my home, would you tell this story to all my friends?" Franz was willing, but unfortunately the invitation never came.

A few weeks later while the main course was being served at a formal dinner at the famous Imperial Hotel in Tokyo with about twenty-five music leaders present, suddenly Horowitz cried out, "Silence! I want everyone to be quiet." When all were quiet, he turned to Franz, "I want you to pray with us as you did when I had dinner at your home. I want you to pray as beautifully as you did then." All listened respectfully as Mohr prayed.

Though Horowitz died without giving any evidence of faith in Christ, Mohr had the opportunity of witnessing on many occasions to him and also to his wife, Toscanini's daughter, because he built bridges. He also had several opportunities to present the gospel to Rubinstein, also Jewish, but without visible response.

Make Jewish evangelism a priority

Even if we live in a community with little or no Jewish population, we should certainly keep abreast of exciting happenings in Jewish evangelism everywhere today.

Moishe Rosen says, "When you tell people the gospel truth, no matter how tactfully, no matter how lovingly, no matter in what form, they always resist it. Sometimes people spit at us. Sometimes they shout at us, shove us or slap us. Comfortable evangelism is like a comfortable cross—rare if it exists. It's tough to get out the gospel. But we keep on witnessing because it works."

Since its beginning, Jews for Jesus has seen over 5000 come to faith through street witnessing campaigns alone, and over 79,000 have asked for further ministry. Jews for Jesus started publishing full-page gospel ads in the secular media back in 1976. They have also published more than 400 different pieces of evangelistic literature in the past 20 years.

Jews for Jesus believes witnessing must be humble, but confrontational and uncompromising. Evangelical missions reject the two-covenant theology which says that though Jesus brought the covenant through which Gentiles come to know the one true God, the Jews already have the covenant through Moses, so that they do not need Jesus the Messiah. That view finds it unnecessary and presumptuous to tell Jews about Jesus. But true evangelical witness would insist on John 14:6, where Jesus Himself said, "I am the way and the truth and the life. No one comes to the Father except through me." Jesus was speaking to Jews when He said those words. "In dealing with the Jewish community," says Rosen, "the issue is whether or not Jesus is the only Savior and whether or not men must confess Him in order to be saved."

The apostle Paul gave priority to the Jews in his missionary endeavors. He said, "I am not ashamed of the gospel, because it is the power of God for the salvation of everyone who believes: first for the Jew, then for the Gentile" (Rom. 1:16). Mitch Glasser, President of Chosen People Ministries, in a lecture at Covenant Theological Seminary, suggested three possible meanings of "first for the Jew." It could be historical priority, describing the order of the presentation of the gospel, first to the Jews, and only later to Gentiles, as was Paul's custom. Or it could be covenant priority since the Jew, recipient of the promise of the gospel, should be the primary audience for gospel preaching. Or it might be present priority in bringing the gospel to the Jews, which the church of every age should acknowledge.

This priority doesn't call for any radical application by evangelists and missionaries and pastors to seek out all the Jews within their sphere of labor before speaking to non-Jews. Such procedure would be difficult, practically impossible. A Fuller Seminary News Release ends with this exhortation: "We feel it incumbent on Christians of all traditions to reinstate the work of Jewish evangelism in their missionary obedience. Jewish oriented programs should be developed. Appropriate agencies for Jewish evangelism should be formed. And churches everywhere should support those existing institutions which are faithfully and lovingly bearing a Christian witness to the Jewish people."

Appreciate the ministry of Messianic Jews

Our hearts should rejoice at the rising number of Jewish believers. We should not force them to divest themselves of their Jewish heritage and culture, nor discourage them from practicing their Jewish customs which are not inconsistent with New Testament truth. Under "News Briefs" in a recent publication of Chosen Peoples Ministries, the number of Messianic congregations in the U.S. was reported at a current estimate of 144—up from only three in 1973; and the number of those attending such congregations up from a handful a generation ago to as many as a possible 150,000 today.

Support Jewish missions financially

Hudson Taylor, founder of the China Inland Mission, used to start every New Year by writing a check to John Wilkinson, founder and director of the Mildmay Mission to the Jews, one of the great Jewish missions of its time, headquartered in England. With the check would invariably be a note, "To the Jew first."

And within the next few days Hudson Taylor would receive a check for the same amount from John Wilkinson with a note, "...and also to the Gentiles."

For many years January was the biggest month for giving to Jewish missions, simply because people took to heart the statement "to the Jew first." One Jewish mission board member told me that large contributions would come from churches and individuals who would say, "We can't evangelize Jews; there are none in our area. So you use this money to witness to the Jews for us."

English Bible teacher Herbert Lockyer put it this way, "By our liberal financial response we seek in some measure to discharge our debt to those we owe so much...a part-payment of a tremendous debt."

FINAL WORDS

William Norman Ewer once wrote this provocative line,

" How odd of God to choose the Jews."

Some years later Cecile Browne added this insightful comment,

" But not so odd
As those who choose a Jewish God
But spurn the Jews."

We owe the Jew a mammoth debt. No room exists for any boasting on our part for any seeming superior position we now possess. Paul reminds us that when we, wild Gentile branches, are grafted into the original olive tree with its strong Jewish roots, *the branches do not support the root, but the root supports the branches* (Rom. 11:18). Gentile branches should be grateful for the nourishment and support from the root of Israel.

In a newsletter Moishe Rosen tells what one elderly woman said to Zola Levitt, TV teacher and advocate for Israel, about her year's missionary service in Israel. Standing there, 80 years young, 100 pounds and spunky, asked by Zola why she had gone to Israel, the woman responded, "You know, I've always been convicted that I have a joy of the prophets of the Jewish Bible and of the Jewish Messiah, but I owe Israel." She then quoted from Romans where Paul explained why he took an offering from the Gentiles in

Greece to starving Jews in Jerusalem. "For if the Gentiles have been partakers of their (Jewish) spiritual things, their duty (Gentiles) is also to minister to them (Jews) in material things" (15:25-27).

She continued, "I ought to return to God's chosen people in material things, but I have no material things, so what I did was send myself. I went to the Israelis and said I can help. I can do this and I can do that, and I went over and I gave one year. That's not much time. I've had 80 years. But I wanted to return something, so I returned my hands and myself."

NOTES

1. Douglas Young, *The Bride and the Wife* (Minneapolis: Free Church Publications, 1959), p. 26.
2. Calvin B. Hanson, *A Gentile With the Heart of a Jew* (Nyack, NY: Parson Publishing, 1979).
3. Yechiel Eckstein, *What Christians Should Know About Jews and Judaism* (Dallas: Word Publishing, 1984), pp. 227-249.
4. Robert Eisenberg, *Boychiks in the Hood* (San Francisco: Harper Collins, 1996), pp. 1-7.
5. Daniel Juster, *Jewish Roots*, pp. 295-296.
6. David Larsen, *Jews*, p. 91.
7. Ibid., p. 331.
8. Gay Block and Malka Drucker, *Rescuers: Portraits of Moral Courage in the Holocaust* (New York: Holmes & Meier Publishers, Inc., 1992).
9. *Newsweek*, April 20, 1998, p.32.
10. David Larsen, p. 53.

11. David H. Stern, *Messianic*, p. 57.

12. Moishe Rosen and Ceil Rosen, *Witnessing to the Jews* (San Francisco: Purple Pomegranate Productions, 1998), p. 5.

13. Franz Mohr and Edith Schaeffer, *My Life with the Great Pianists* (Grand Rapids: Baker Books, 1992), pp. 54-159.

Other Books to Enrich Your Life

Positive Attitudes for the 50+ Years: *How Anyone Can Make Them Happy & Fulfilling* - *Willard A. Scofield*

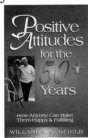

Willard Scofield, former associate editor for *Decision* magazine, counselor at Peale Center for Christian Living, and Baptist missionary, addresses 75 concerns of Christians 50 years and older. His hope-filled responses will change negative attitudes into positive thoughts and actions as he shares practical and spiritual insights from the Scriptures. A great gift idea for parents and grandparents!
ISBN 0-9654806-2-3   paper $12.00

Yes We Can Love One Another! *Catholics & Protestants Can Share A Common Faith* - *Warren Angel*

Christ's Church cannot be seen in disharmony and acrimony, for Jesus prayed that His disciples would be one in love. Evangelical minister Warren Angel shows us how Catholic and Protestant believers can love one another by understanding their common bond in Jesus Christ, and by breaking down misconceptions and false barriers to fellowship and mission. Then, in love, we can be a Church of power and joy in the Holy Spirit. A book for all traditions!
ISBN 0-9654806-0-7   paper $12.00

Jesus in the Image of God
A Challenge to Christlikeness - *Leslie B. Flynn*

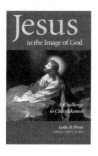

An antidote to the views of the Jesus Seminar! The real Jesus of the Gospels was a King among men who, though often abused and vilified, denied Himself to serve the poor, the sick, the sinful, and the outcast with a loving heart and healing ministry – God's own nature and likeness. Jesus still challenges us to become like Him. Can we do this? Should we even try? Leslie Flynn says *YES* and shows us how!
ISBN 0-9654806-1-5   paper $12.00

Available at Your Favorite Bookstore
or Call: 1-800-463-7818
Magnus Press, P.O. Box 2666, Carlsbad, CA 92018